"Welcome... to England's Story.
I have written this book primarily to
interest children in the 7-11 age group,
to help them understand the narrative
of our country's history."

"Twins Sam and Nikki discover,
by questioning their grandfather, all
about the main events of the last 2000 years.
Whether you are young, or 'young in mind'
I hope you will enjoy the experience."

PUBLISHED BY
TEST VALLEY CHURCHES BOOK SOCIETY
27, The Avenue
Andover
Hampshire. SP10 3EP
01264 365190

PRINTED AND BOUND BY
ADVENT COLOUR Ltd.
19, East Portway
Andover
Hampshire. SP10 3LU
01264 359359

ISBN 978-0-9556631-5-4

THE AUTHOR'S PERSONAL ACKNOWLEDGEMENTS

Rt. Hon. Sir George Young Bt. CH. MP.
for his support and encouragement of this publication.

Jane Pleydell-Bouverie MA (Oxon) and the festival committee of Chalke Valley History Trust.
Tom Holland MA (Cantab) for his kindness in writing the Foreword to this book.
David Holdaway for his specialist advice and essential typesetting skills.
Adam De Marco and Steve Berry of Advent Colour Ltd.
Mrs. Sheila Hindle BA Hons. for her suggested refinements to the first two drafts.
Miss Charlotte Fry for her design of the title lettering.
My dearest wife Diana for her customary, careful proof-reading.

BIBLIOGRAPHY

A History of the English-speaking Peoples .... Winston.S.Churchill.
Set in a Silver Sea .... Arthur Bryant.
The Isles .... Norman Davies.

From 55 BC to 2013

A History of England for young minds

WRITTEN

and

ILLUSTRATED

by

BRYAN BEGGS

With my best wishes

16 FEB 2017

'A nation that forgets its past has no future'
WINSTON CHURCHILL

FIRST EDITION

CONTENTS

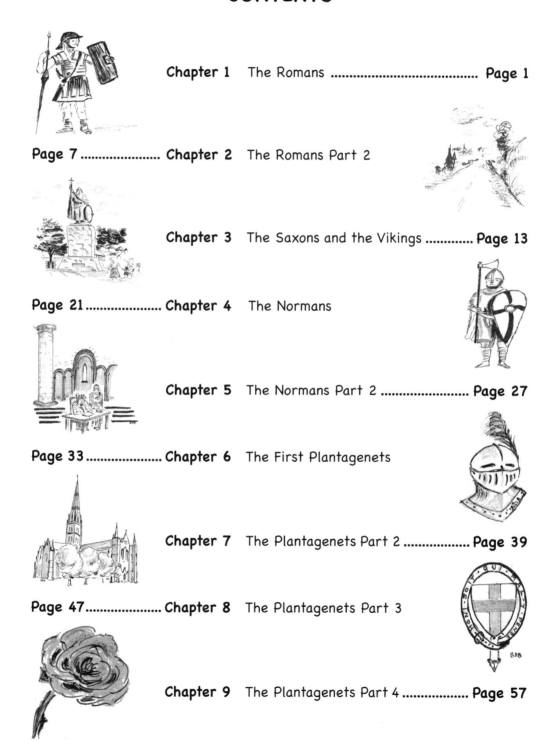

CONTENTS

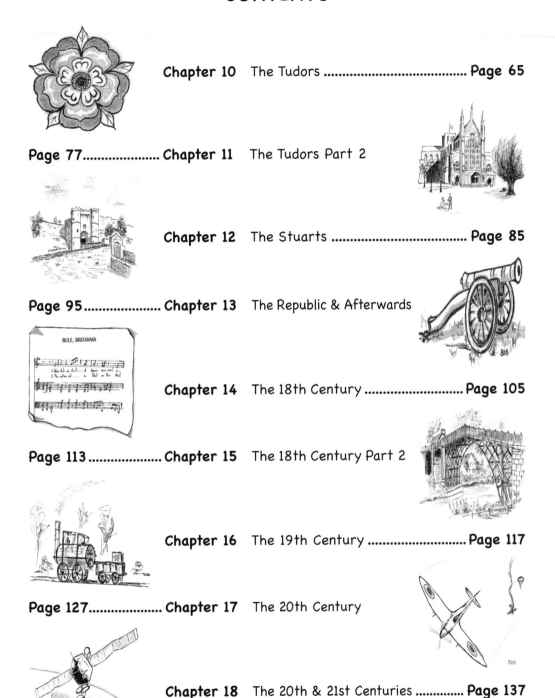

This book is dedicated to the fond memory of
Mrs. Patricia Betty Rayer
1915-2013
of Ladysmith, Vancouver Island, B.C. Canada
and her elder sister
Mrs Norah May Walker
1909-1999
of West Wickham, Kent.

Gentle English ladies and aunts of the author, who were the
daughters of Mr.& Mrs W.B. Douglas,
and who lived during their youth
at 'Sunningdale',
Commonside,
Keston,
Kent.

LONDON

21st November 2013

FOREWORD
By
Tom Holland
Author and Historian

As an Honorary patron of the Chalke Valley History Festival, and a trustee of the Chalke Valley History Trust, I was delighted to be asked to contribute the foreword to this book. In recent years, the trust has been anxious to foster an interest in our country's history among younger children. This book should help to do just that.

Last year, the festival decided for the first time to focus on visitors of school age. Over 1000 students from both the state and independent sectors attended their own two-day festival on our site. We will be laying on a similar event in 2014 – only bigger and better, and with a third day for Primary Schools.

How lucky we are, then, that local author Bryan Beggs should have published his book this year, with the same aims as the Trust – and how incredibly generous of him to have donated the entire proceeds from the first edition to the Chalke Valley History Trust. All parents who want to share the excitements and wonders of English history with their children will be grateful to Bryan for having written this book – just as all children who read it are in for a treat!

'Sam and his twin sister Nikki were with their grandfather
in the sitting room of his home… it was raining outside…'

CHAPTER 1

THE ROMANS

The Beginnings of England 55 BC – AD 43

Sam and his twin sister Nikki were with their grandfather in the sitting-room of his home... it was raining outside...

Suddenly Sam said, "Grandpa, when did England begin?"

"Well that's quite a difficult question to answer actually," began his grandfather, "but I ..."

"Grandpa, do you know how it got its name?" interrupted Nikki.

"One question at a time please, you two," replied their grandfather, "but yes, I can answer your question Nikki at once... the word 'England' came from 'Angle-land'. The Angles were a people who came here, from the part of Europe where today Denmark joins on to Germany. They came after the Romans went back to Europe in about AD 410. They built their farms and homes mostly in the north and east of our country... we still call the counties of Norfolk, Suffolk, Cambridgeshire and Essex, 'East Anglia' as

you probably know. If one of you will bring me the atlas from the bookshelf over there, I will show you exactly where it is on the map."

"They must have had to come over the sea," said Sam, looking at the map.

The Atlas

"Certainly they did," said his grandfather, "and the boats they used would seem very small to us by today's standards, and therefore their journey could be quite dangerous."

"... but I think you said the Romans were here first," said Nikki; "what name did they call our country?"

"Britannia," replied her grandfather.

"That sounds very much like 'Britain'," said Sam. "We call our country 'Great' Britain, don't we?" he added. Then he thought for a moment and said, "Does the word 'Great' mean 'really good and wonderful', Grandpa?"

1

"No, I'm afraid not... even though <u>we</u> may think it is! I must tell you that the word 'great' really means England and a <u>great</u> bit more... by which is meant, 'including Wales and Scotland'."

"Oh, that <u>is</u> interesting," said Sam, "I've always wondered about that. So it was Britannia first, then Angleland, then England and then part of Great Britain. "

"Quite right."

"Perhaps I should have asked you, when did 'Britain' begin?" Sam continued.

"Well, it would have been easier for me to give you an answer," replied his grandfather. Would you like me to tell you a bit more about 'Britannia' and when the Romans came here?"

Ooo, yes please Grandpa," said both the children.

"Well then, I think the first Roman person I should tell you about, is a general called Julius Caesar."

"I think I've heard that name," said Nikki.

"Good. He first came to our country in the year 55 BC, but he did not stay very long and came back again the following year. Can either of you tell me what year that would have been?"

Julius Caesar landing his legions in Kent 54 BC

"54 BC I think," said Nikki

"Quite correct... did you think the same Sam?"

"Yes Grandpa and the next year after that was 53 BC."

"Very good!"

"Will you tell us about 'BC and AD', and why Julius Caesar came, please Grandpa?" asked Nikki.

"I certainly will, but I think I will begin, with the answer to your second question. In fact there were probably several reasons why he came here... certainly he was invited by the son of a tribal king who lived in Essex, and who wanted Caesar's help to get revenge on the king of a neighbouring tribe, who had killed his father. I expect another reason might have been that even though he was already famous for conquering 'Gaul' [what we call France today]; he may have wanted even more fame and riches. "

"How many tribes were there living in Britannia, Grandpa?" asked Sam.

"At least twenty."

"That seems quite a lot," said Nikki.

"Yes, it does, but you must understand that their ancestors had come from other places in Europe in the thousands of years that had gone before... some had probably <u>walked</u> into this land soon after the ice-age and before the English Channel was formed about 8000 years ago, and although I will tell you some of the tribal names, you don't need to try to remember them. One of the most interesting ones lived in the south of our country, they were called the Belgae; part of the same tribe lived in Gaul and so they used to trade with each other."

A Roman coin

"Trading was mostly swopping things wasn't it?" asked Nikki.

"Yes it was," replied her grandfather, "but money in the form of coins was becoming more usual. Often when people dig to discover Roman things they find a coin and this helps them to give a date to other things they find in the same place."

"Is it because the coins have kings' heads on them?" asked Sam.

"Yes, and even the <u>names</u> of the kings or emperors," added his grandfather... "now, I haven't forgotten about 'BC and AD', but there's a bit more I want to tell you about Julius Caesar."

"You said he was already famous for conquering Gaul," said Sam, "so how many soldiers did he have?"

"Quite a large number, but he only brought two legions with him on his first visit in 55 BC... two legions was about 10,000 men. He first landed in Kent. Almost at once there was a storm and many of his ships were wrecked. So he didn't stay long. The next year he returned to Kent again but this time with five legions, and that expedition needed about 800 ships to ferry them across the sea. The Kentish tribes knew they could not defeat such a large number so they made peace with Julius Caesar and offered to give him money and hostages if he would go away again... which he did, after defeating the tribe who had killed the king of Essex."

"What happened to him after he left Britain, Grandpa?" asked Nikki.

"Well, he went back to Gaul for a few years and then he was ordered by the authorities in Rome to disband his army, which he did not want to do. In 49 BC he marched his army across a small stream in Italy called the Rubicon, which was considered to be treason against the Roman Republic. However, he defeated his enemies in Rome and looked like becoming the first Roman emperor, but in 44 BC some of his former friends murdered him to prevent such a thing happening."

Death of Julius Caesar

"The Romans did come here again didn't they?" asked Sam.

"Oh yes, but nearly one hundred years went by before that happened," replied his grandfather.

"So when exactly was that please Grandpa?" asked Nikki.

"In AD 43, and strangely enough for almost exactly the same reasons as the first time... in other words they were asked to come. Now I think I ought to explain about 'BC and AD'."

"Could you tell us who decided when BC changed to AD," said Sam.

"Well no one actually decided it... it sort of, just happened," replied his grandfather, "but it is normally credited to an English monk called Bede, who wrote a history of the English church in the year AD 731. He decided to date the events in his book according to the year of the birth of Jesus, and gradually over the next hundreds of years other writers did the same... by about AD 1500 all the European countries were using the same system."

"Was there a year zero?" asked Nikki.

"No there wasn't; after 1 BC came AD 1."

"What does AD stand for please?" asked Sam.

"Anno Domini, and that is Latin [the Roman language] for 'the year of the Lord'... meaning the year of Jesus' birth... B.C. stands for 'before Christ'."

"Did Bede actually know the year of Jesus birth?" asked Nikki.

"No he didn't," replied her grandfather, "but he knew that some other scholars had tried to work it out from information about the rulers of that time, such as Augustus and Herod, and we now know that they were almost correct... the best guess for Jesus' birth is about 5 BC. You remember that the 'three wise men' or 'three kings' came to find Jesus and they met King Herod?"

"Yes Grandpa," said both the children.

"Well it is known that Herod died in 4 BC, so that helps us to know that Jesus must have been born before that date; and we can be <u>more</u> certain that he died on the cross in AD 33."

"That means he must have been about thirty-seven when he died I think," said Sam.

"Yes, I agree," said his grandfather. "Now I think I ought to tell you a bit more about Roman Britain, don't you?"

"Perhaps you could tell us a bit about some of the places, and if they are still here today," suggested Nikki.

1. Winchester   2. St. Albans
3. Colchester

"Right, let's get the map again and see what we can find... there is Winchester... and there St. Albans.... and somewhere... look just there, Colchester, which was the most important of them all, when the Romans came again in AD 43."

"I've found Colchester," said Sam, "it's in Essex; was it more important than London?"

"Very much so," replied his grandfather. "In fact London did not really exist at this time, and even the other two places were really no more than tribal camps, whereas Colchester had become a focus for trade with Europe and had a king. Coins have been found that date the earliest king's reign in that area, to between 25 BC and 15 BC... so therefore it was probably the first real town in Britain."

"Didn't you say Grandpa, that when the Romans came back again it was for the same reason that Julius Caesar had come in 54 BC?" asked Sam.

"Yes it was. The king in Colchester died in AD 42 and there was a dispute between his sons as to who should succeed him; the eldest went to Gaul and asked the new Roman emperor Claudius to help him regain his lands. The emperor agreed because it suited him to be associated with a victory in Britain, which he thought he would be able to ensure. Therefore he sent a general with four legions to Britain with orders to inform him when he could come to see the battle for Colchester... this all happened as I've said, in AD 43."

"Did the Romans win?" asked Nikki.

"Yes they did; their four legions were very good troops and they had elephants with them too, which must have made the British tribesmen very afraid indeed. The emperor got his victory and declared that Colchester should become a real Roman town, and so the first permanent base for Romans troops was built there. I think this is probably the best place for me to stop for the moment, because the story of England for the next 400 years is very much the story of the Roman occupation."

"Does Queen Boadicea come into the story soon?" asked Nikki.

"Yes she does."

"I wish we could go on a bit more," said Sam.

"Not today, but perhaps tomorrow, if you still want me to do so," replied their grandfather.

A Roman soldier

CHAPTER 2

THE ROMANS Part 2

The Roman province of Britannia AD 43 – AD 410

"Sam we're ready," called Nikki.

"I'm coming; I'm just getting the atlas in case we need it."

"Good idea," said their grandfather, "I expect we will."

The children sat either side of their grandfather on the sofa... "Now where shall we begin...? I think you mentioned Queen Boadicea last time, didn't you Nikki?"

"Yes, Grandpa."

"...and you told us about the battle at Colchester where the Roman legions had elephants to help them," said Sam.

"Oh yes, I remember... some time after the battle had been fought and the Roman town was beginning to take shape, the four legions marched off in different directions and began to subdue all the tribes they met, so that in just four years the Romans controlled all of Britannia from Exeter in the west to Lincoln in the north. As they went they built roads [the Romans were great road builders] and military camps. Of course roads are fine until you come to a wide and deep river... what do you think they had to do then?"

"Build a bridge?" said Sam.

"Yes. Where do you think the best place might be?" asked his grandfather.

"Where the river is easy to cross and the bridge does not have to be too big, I should think," answered Nikki.

"That's quite right," replied her grandfather, "let's imagine you are a Roman soldier walking from the coast of Kent or Sussex to Colchester, what's the biggest river you have to cross?" They all looked at the map of England in the atlas... "The Thames!" said Sam.

"Correct," said grandfather. "The place they chose was near where they had waded across to fight the tribes defending Colchester... it was the place we call London today. The first London Bridge was built in AD 50. Eventually all the most important Roman roads led to or from the bridge at

Possible example of the first Roman London Bridge

Londinium [the name the Romans gave to the place] so it hasn't changed much since then has it?"

"No, that will be quite easy to remember," said Nikki... "But what about Queen Boadicea?"

"I'm just coming to that," replied her grandfather. "For about ten years the Romans did not try to conquer any more of the parts of Britannia, but then a new governor decided to attack the tribe living in North Wales and he took with him two of the four legions [the other two were based in Gloucester and Lincoln] so there were almost no troops left to guard Colchester and London. This would probably have been all right if the friendly king of the Iceni tribe, who lived where Norfolk is today, had not died. After his death, his queen, Boadicea and her tribe, were treated very badly by the Romans who were in charge there... in AD 60 they decided to attack the Romans and so they marched down to Colchester, which they easily captured, killing many of the people there and destroying the new Roman buildings.

Queen Boadicea and her tribe attacking Colchester

Then they went to London and did the same, and then the same again to the Roman camp at St. Albans. The Roman governor heard about the attacks by Boadicea and eventually marched with his two legions back from North Wales and managed to defeat her. The queen drank poison to avoid being captured, and most of her forces were killed."

"Gosh! That's amazing," said Sam, "I wonder what would have happened if Queen Boadicea had won?"

A Roman Road ...today

"One thing is sure," replied his grandfather, "England would have been very different... in the first place all those roads we were talking about would probably not have been built."

"Are some of the Roman roads still in use?" asked Sam.

"They certainly are; wherever you are in England today there will be a Roman road not far away."

"Can we walk on one?" asked Nikki.

"Yes you can... and drive along them in cars too! They are usually very straight and I'm sure I can show you some on the map... let's look shall we?"

"Grandpa, were there any other tribal leaders that fought against the Romans?" asked Sam.

"Yes, mostly they were in the north of the country, and it took the Romans a long time to overcome them. It was another Julius, Julius Agricola, the governor for six years from AD 78, who managed finally to extend the Roman province right up into where Scotland is today, but the hills and mountains always made it easy for the tribes to attack the Romans, so eventually when Hadrian became emperor in AD 117, he decided that a frontier had to be established and so when he came to Britannia in AD 122, he ordered..."

"I know, I know," said Nikki interrupting, "it was Hadrian's Wall."

"Yes, yes... the famous Hadrian's Wall; and it's still there today. Did you know that another wall was built by Hadrian's son?"

"No, Grandpa," said Sam,"where was that?"

Hadrian's Wall

"It was much further to the north, roughly between where Edinburgh and Glasgow are today. Since Hadrian's adopted son was called Antoninus Pius, it was given the name of the 'Antonine Wall', but it was soon abandoned after the emperor died and the frontier remained at Hadrian's Wall until the Romans left Britannia in AD 410."

"Please can we go there one day?" asked Nikki.

"I expect so," replied their grandfather, "I have to say that I've not been there myself, so it will be very interesting for me too. There are museums of things that archaeologists have found when doing their "digs", and almost every year more and more information of how the Roman soldiers lived in their camps seems to be discovered."

"Did any other Roman emperors come to Britannia, Grandpa?" asked Sam.

"Seven, I think, replied his grandfather, "but there was always a lot of fighting between the Romans themselves whenever an emperor died or was killed, and many only ruled for a few months, so there was hardly time for them to come over here! One that I must tell you about was Constantine; he lived between about AD 274 and AD 337. He came with his father, who was a sort of vice-emperor 'in the west'."

"Like a vice-president," enquired Sam.

"Yes that's right. In AD 293 the Roman emperor Diocletian decided that the empire needed two emperors, one to administer the eastern provinces and, he himself, would manage the western ones including Britannia. His plan was that each emperor would have a deputy called a 'Caesar'. Constantine's father was the Caesar of the western empire. When Constantine's father died in York in AD 306, his troops at once decided that they wanted Constantine to lead them and so they proclaimed him 'emperor', but rather like Julius Caesar before him, Constantine had to fight several battles with rivals over many years before he finally became the one and only emperor in AD 324."

"Did he build any walls?" asked Nikki.

"No, but he did build some Christian churches", replied her grandfather, "and was very tolerant of the Christian religion; in fact Christianity became the official religion of the Roman Empire during his rule…. now, I could stop here; anyone ready for a drink?"

"I'd like a drink, but I would like it better if you can tell us the rest of the story please," said Nikki.

Roman walls and turrets at Portchester

"I can wait too," said Sam.

"Well there's not a great deal more to tell you, so you won't have to wait too long," said their grandfather. "Even before Constantine became the emperor there had been raids upon the coastal settlements of Britannia by the Saxons, and so the Romans had built strong defensive walls around their main ports and had set up a fleet of warships to protect them. In Europe also, the attacks by other peoples on the Roman provinces under later rulers caused similar problems and gradually the legions in Britannia were taken away to defend the frontiers elsewhere; by AD 410 they had all gone."

"Was that the end of the Romans in Britannia?" asked Sam.

"Yes it was; they never came back again. There were of course ordinary British and Roman citizens in the country, and an attempt was made to continue their normal lives and to set up a sort of 'Home Guard'. A British leader called Vortigern invited some Saxons to come and defend them against other Saxons, but it didn't really work and the near neighbours of the Saxons, the Angles and the Jutes, also came in increasing numbers."

"I remember you telling us about 'Angleland', was this the time they came?" he asked.

"Yes it was. Slowly but surely they drove the Britons back towards the western parts of the land; the Roman towns became derelict and the villas and houses were abandoned."

"How sad," said Nikki, "is that where we stop today?"

"I think it would be quite a good place, replied her grandfather. Next time I shall tell you about how the Saxons themselves became the victims of another invasion from the sea... I'm sure you've heard of the Vikings."

"That sounds exciting,"said Sam "I can't wait!"

"Now, it's drinks for all of us I think... who wants what?"

An abandoned Roman villa

CHAPTER 3

THE SAXONS and THE VIKINGS

The first English Kingdoms AD 430–1035

A couple of days went by before the children visited their grandparents again, and they had hardly come through the door before Sam said," When can we start the story of the Saxons please Grandpa?"

"Perhaps after tea, because I think Granny is planning a rather special trip for us all this afternoon."

"Ooo! Where to?" asked Nikki.

"To Winchester I believe," replied her grandfather, "one of the things we'll be able to see there is the huge statue of the Saxon king, Alfred the Great."

"That will be really <u>great</u>," said Sam with a bit of a grin.

So it was, that much later, after tea, the children were able to ask their grandfather to continue the next part of the story of England.

"Now where shall I start... can you remind me of where we got to?" he asked.

"The Roman legions had all gone back to Gaul and other places... I think it was by AD 410," said Sam.

"... and the people in Britannia had invited some Saxons to come and protect them against other Saxons," said Nikki, "I think the plan did not work," she added.

"Ah, yes, thank you both," said their grandfather. "No, the plan certainly did not work. One of the groups came in about AD 430 and was led by Hengist and Horsa. They were first allowed to stay on the island of Thanet, which is part of Kent, but soon they realised they could almost do whatever they wanted and so, helped by more Saxon invaders and their neighbours from Jutland, before long they were in control of the whole of Kent."

"What happened to the British and Roman people?" asked Nikki.

"Some, as I said before, fled away towards Wales and the West Country, others buried their treasures and followed the legions back to Gaul," said her grandfather.

King Alfred's statue …Winchester

"What sort of treasures, Grandpa?" asked Sam.

"Beautiful silver things like plates and wine jugs, and money of course. You can see examples of the sorts of things that have been discovered, in the British Museum. I expect they hoped one day to come back and dig them up again."

"Gosh, I'd like to find some buried treasure," said Sam.

"You'll have to save up and buy a metal-detector then, like the man who found the hoard of gold items in a field just to the north of Winchester in the year 2000," replied his grandfather.

"How long did it take for the Saxons, Angles and Jutes to dominate the British, Grandpa?" asked Nikki.

The Winchester Hoard …one of the gold Torcs

"About a hundred years."

"That's a long time," said Sam.

"It is, and there were times when the Saxons were beaten back. You remember the 'Round Table' we saw on the wall of Winchester Castle, which shows the names of King Arthur and all his knights?"

"Yes."

"Well, although the stories of King Arthur were mostly 'made up' about 1000 years later than this time, there actually was a British chieftain, who fought and won a great battle against the Saxons near where Swindon is today, in about AD 500. In fact he probably won several battles and prevented the Saxons and Angles from extending their territory for quite some time, and so the stories about him later became the 'Legend of King Arthur'."

"Wow!" said Sam. "So when was the round table made that we saw today?"

"About the middle of the 14th Century... what date do you think that was?"

"Fourteenth century, means it must have been 13... something," said Sam.

"Quite correct," replied his grandfather, "so we might say 1350 for example."

The Round Table in Winchester Castle

"How do people know when it was made," asked Nikki.

"There are ways of matching the growth rings found in the wood of the table with a scientific database of tree rings that has only recently been established and which can date trees going back many thousands of years," said her grandfather. "Now, don't you think we ought to go back to the Saxons again?"

"Yes please," they both replied.

"During the next hundred years from AD 500, the Saxons became the dominant people... the East Saxons lived in Essex; the south Saxons in Sussex, and the west Saxons in Wessex. They were what we call pagan people, that is to say they were not of the Christian religion, which you may remember was made the official religion of the Roman Empire by the Emperor Constantine, about two hundred years before. Eventually the pagan king of Kent married a Christian princess from Gaul and allowed her to bring some Christian monks with her to England. The king, Ethelbert, gave the monks an old chapel in Canterbury, once used in Roman times, for a church, then in AD 597 the Pope sent Augustine and some other monks to try to see if they could re-establish the Christian religion again in Kent and perhaps throughout England. After meeting and hearing Augustine, Ethelbert himself became a Christian and gradually other Saxons did the same, first in Kent then in London and Essex, and later the Angles in Northumbria did the same. By the way, from this time onwards in my story, I'm going to call all the inhabitants of England, 'Anglo-Saxons'."

"Did the Anglo-Saxons all become Christians?" asked Sam.

"I think mostly they did, or at least their kings did; and you should know that there had always been Christians in those places where some of the British people had gone when the Saxons first came, by which I mean Wales and the West Country. Christianity also became established in Ireland by AD 500, through the ministry of St. Patrick."

"How do we know about this, Grandpa?" asked Nikki.

"Mostly we have to thank Bede and all the other Christian monasteries where the first books were slowly and carefully made. Remember Bede wrote his book about the history of the church in England in AD 731, which

The ruins of Jarrow Monastery, the home of Bede

was the time when the kingdom of Northumbria was the most important of the Anglo-Saxon kingdoms and Bede lived in a monastery at Jarrow."

"Can you tell us what other kingdoms there were in England?" said Sam.

"Well, they changed quite a bit according to the powerfulness of their individual kings," explained his grandfather, "a good example is that Mercia became the most important in AD 757, when it was ruled by King Offa."

"Did he make any good offers?" asked Sam.

"No, I don't think so," said his grandfather, smiling, "this king spelt his name, O * F * F * A... Nikki, you'll be pleased to know that he built a long wall."

"Ooo, where was that Grandpa?"

"Almost all along the boundary that now separates England from Wales."

"How long was it Grandpa?" said Sam.

"At least 100 miles, but it was only ever what is called an 'earthwork', it was never a stone rampart like Hadrian's Wall; today we call it Offa's Dyke and there is a footpath along its entire length. Offa was the first king to call himself 'The King of the Angles'."

"Where was 'Mercia' Grandpa?" asked Nikki.

"Very roughly it was all the middle of England."

"Excuse me Grandpa, but didn't you say you were going to tell us about the Vikings?" said Sam.

"I did, and it's funny you should ask me now, because the Vikings first landed in England almost at the end of the reign of King Offa. They landed near where Weymouth is today in the year AD 789. Four years later they attacked the monastery on Lindisfarne on the north-east coast."

"I shall remember that,7.8.9 is easy... but where did they come from?" asked Nikki.

"From Norway and Denmark. In the beginning they usually attacked the monasteries because that was where the valuable treasures were kept, and the monks who lived in the monasteries were not the sort of people used to fighting."

"They had to come across the deep sea," said Sam.

"Yes, quite right, however their ships were very well built and they managed to sail not only to the nearest coasts of our country, but also around the north of Scotland to Ireland and the Isle of Man."

Viking invasion

"After sailing here did they just stay?" asked Nikki.

"No," replied her grandfather, "they generally took their stolen things back to their homelands just like the Saxons had done when they first came... then after AD 865 they too stayed here and came to dominate the Anglo-Saxons in the north and east of the country. In the south and west they came up against the strong Saxon kingdom of Wessex ruled by Alfred, whose statue we saw today. He defeated them and they made peace with Alfred, and the country was divided more or less in half between the two groups along a line roughly between London and Manchester. One of the terms of peace that Alfred insisted upon, was that their king should become a Christian."

"Did they only come to the British Isles?" asked Sam.

"No, they attacked cities in Germany and France and even sailed round into the Mediterranean Sea. The peace in England lasted until AD 910, when the Viking settlers also called 'The Danes' tried again to attack Wessex, but they were defeated in a great battle by King Alfred's son, Edward the Elder; he then took advantage of their defeat to extend his own control over all their lands to the south of the Humber river... look, there is the river Humber on the map."

"That's almost the same area that the Romans conquered when they first came here," said Sam.

"Yes, it was... and later when Edward's son Athelstan became king [again just like the Romans] he conquered the rest of the Danish and Viking lands right up into Scotland. On his coins he had inscribed in the old Roman language of Latin 'REX TOTIUS BRITANNIAE' which means 'King of the whole of Britain'. Athelstan and his son Edgar were called the first kings of 'Engla-land'. If you remember Sam, the first question you asked me was 'when did England begin'...I think most people would answer you, 'when Edgar was king'."

"Once Engla-land became England, was that the end of the Vikings?" asked Nikki.

"No, I'm afraid it was not. They stayed away while England had her strong Saxon kings, but when they discovered at the end of the 10th century that England had a weak king, who was called Ethelred-the-Unready, they came back. Ethelred gave them money to go away when they threatened him with war, but they kept coming back asking for more and more money, and making war anyway! Life for the ordinary people was awful and eventually Ethelred ran away to France and a Danish king, called Sweyn, whose sister had been killed by Ethelred, came and took over the land. When Sweyn died in 1013, Ethelred came back and fought Sweyn's son, Canute, to decide who should be king."

"I've heard of King Canute," said Nikki, "he sat at the edge of the sea, or something."

"Do you know why he sat there?" asked her grandfather.

"I'm afraid I can't remember."

"He wanted to teach his courtiers a lesson... he wanted to show them that he was not as powerful as they kept on telling him

King Canute

he was. To prove it he sat at the edge of the sea and ordered the tide not to come in [knowing of course that it would], hoping that his friends would get the message. He was a religious king, who encouraged the Christian church and of all the lands he ruled he liked England the best."

"What happened to Ethelred?" asked Sam.

"He died in London whilst being besieged by Canute in 1016 and after his son Edmund died later in the same year, King Canute became the undisputed king and married Ethelred's widow, Queen Emma, which helped him to preserve peace with his Anglo-Saxon people. He was crowned king in

London in the original St. Paul's Cathedral and ruled peacefully over our country until 1035."

"Is that the end of the Saxons and Vikings and Danes?" asked Sam.

"Not quite, but I think we ought to stop for a while at this point because your parents will soon be here to collect you... perhaps next week you would like to come again and we will talk about The Normans and their conquest of our country," replied her grandfather.

"I shall look forward to that," said Nikki.

"I already know a bit about The Normans," said Sam, "there was a big battle and a Saxon king called Harold was killed."

" I knew that too," said his sister, "it was in 1066. Grandpa, what happened in the years between Canute and Harold?"

"I'm going to save that until next time, but you could try to find out a bit about another king called Edward the Confessor if you like. He was king in the time you are asking about and he was the person who built Westminster Abbey in London."

"Do you mean the place where Prince William married Kate Middleton," said Nikki.

"Yes indeed, Westminster Abbey is the place where nearly all coronations and royal weddings take place, and inside you can still see the tomb of King Edward the Confessor as well as many other royal tombs... now, that's the front door bell... off you go."

"Thank you Grandpa, we'll come back soon."

Tomb of Edward the Confessor in Westminster Abbey

20

CHAPTER 4

THE NORMANS

Final Saxon years... and William I 1066–1087

The week went by really quickly. Nikki and Sam were soon back at their grandparents house and keen to continue with 'England's Story'.

"Please can you remind me where we got to Grandpa?" asked Sam.

"Well, we are coming close to the invasion of the Normans from France in 1066 and the final defeat of the Anglo-Saxons at the Battle of Hastings. However, I remember I said I would start by explaining what happened after King Canute died in 1035. Canute had children by two different wives, so there was always likely to be trouble between them. Of course, King Ethelred had had children too, so that made things even more complicated. Different groups of people in England supported different claimants to the throne. One of these groups was led by Earl Godwin of Wessex. It happened that both Canute's sons died a few years after their father... Ethelred's eldest son was captured when he came over from France and blinded by Earl Godwin, which left just Ethelred's youngest son Edward, who was a rather weak character and whom Earl Godwin thought he could dominate. He therefore supported him to be the next king. He became known as 'Edward the Confessor'."

"What does 'confessor' mean Grandpa?" asked Nikki.

"Confessor was a nickname, it really means a priest... Edward was a truly religious and pious man, quite unsuited to be a king at such a turbulent time. Earl Godwin was the man with the real power, he even persuaded the king to marry his daughter."

"Grandpa, last time you told us that Edward the Confessor built Westminster Abbey," said Sam."

"He did, and although the abbey we see in London today has changed a lot, as I told you, his tomb is still there."

"I couldn't find out anything about Edward the Confessor," said Nikki, "but I did find out that Westminster Abbey has the tomb of the 'Unknown Soldier'."

"It does indeed, but that is of course recent history and I must just tell you a bit more about the reign of Edward the Confessor. Just like today in our parliament where there are political parties, there were different factions in Edward's court, the Anglo-Saxons, the Anglo-Danish and the Normans."

"I didn't think we were quite up to the Normans yet," said Sam.

"No, not quite," agreed his grandfather, "but Edward had grown up in Normandy and he gave some important positions of power to his Norman friends. So when Edward died in 1066 there were at least three different groups who thought one of their own group should be the next king."

"Did Edward have any children?" asked Sam.

"No, he did not. However, it is believed that he may have promised the throne both to his wife's brother Harold Godwinson, and also to William, Duke of Normandy, so there was a quarrel between those two, which eventually was resolved by William's invasion of England and Harold's defeat at the famous Battle of Hastings in 1066... shall I stop here?"

"Oh, no, not yet Grandpa... please," said Nikki, "it's getting to an interesting part!"

William I landing at Pevensey Bay 1066

"Well, just a little bit more," replied their grandfather..." I think I ought to go back a little... did I tell you about the earlier invasion that year?"

"No, I don't think so."

"Of all the claimants to the throne when Edward died, the only one in England at the time was Harold, the son of Earl Godwin, and he was crowned king on 6th June 1066. The other claimants, William of Normandy and the King of Norway each planned invasions. The first to arrive was the group from Norway and they landed in Yorkshire. Harold marched north and defeated them, but no sooner had he done so, than he got the news that William had landed in Sussex. He rushed back to deal with the new threat and after collecting extra troops in London, he continued towards the south coast to block William's path. Although the battle that followed is called the Battle of Hastings, it was actually fought a few miles inland where the town of Battle is today."

"So it ought to be called the Battle of Battle then," said Nikki.

"Yes, I suppose it should, but at that time the nearest town was in fact Hastings, and so that's why it retains that name today."

"They were always having battles weren't they?" said Sam.

"Yes, it was a very rough time indeed," agreed his grandfather, "fighting was almost the normal way of settling disputes."

"How long did the Battle of Hastings last?" asked Nikki.

"Nearly all day, and Harold and his men might easily have won, but the Normans pretended to run away and then the Anglo-Saxons rushed down from the high hill where they had fought for so long, and the Normans on their horses then turned round and killed them. Do you know how King Harold died?"

"Yes, I do," said Sam, "he was killed by an arrow in his eye."

"I knew that too," said Nikki.

"I'm sure you did," said her grandfather, "but did you know that William built an abbey on the battlefield and over the place where Harold died?"

"No... is it still there?"

The ruins of Battle Abbey today

"Yes it is, one day we will go there. Now at last we have come to what is called 'The Norman Conquest'. After being crowned in London as king, William, gradually over the next years, was able to conquer all the land of England... of course, being still Duke of Normandy he had to defend and look after his lands in France too."

"I suppose he had to sail to and fro' across The Channel," said Sam.

"He certainly did, for his eldest son Robert, whom he had left in charge over there, rebelled against him, and no sooner had he sorted things out in Normandy, than there was another rebellion against him in England."

"He was always fighting it seems to me," said Nikki.

"He did have time to do other things... towards the end of his life he ordered a list to be made of all the property in England, so that he could find out how much money he should have and who owned the land.

The Domesday Book and 'Little Domesday'

This was done amazingly quickly in 1086 and the results were put into two volumes of a large book... later they became known as 'The Domesday Book', and you can see them today at the National Archives offices in Kew in Surrey."

"Did he build any walls?" asked Nikki.

"If you mean, like Hadrian's Wall, then the answer is, no... but the Normans were very great builders of castles and cathedrals, and you can still see them all over the country. Seven of our most famous cathedrals were started before William died in 1087. One of the most famous castles is the 'White Tower' in the centre of what is today called the 'Tower of London'."

"We've been there," said Sam and Nikki together, "and we saw the crown jewels in a building near the White Tower."

"I'm sure you would have enjoyed that," replied their grandfather.

"Grandpa, it can't have been building castles and fighting all the time surely?"

"No, it wasn't... laws were made and judges appointed and something called the 'Feudal System', which was the way things were done in France, was introduced into England."

"What was that?" asked Sam.

"It was a social system whereby everyone owed a duty to their lord, based upon the land they owned, and the lords owed a duty to the king, from whom they had received their lands."

THE WHITE TOWER … The Tower of London

"Did you say William died in 1087?" asked Nikki.

"I did."

"Then what happened Grandpa?" she continued.

"I'm afraid to say that once again there was a lot of fighting amongst his sons. William I had given their homeland of Normandy to his eldest son Robert, and he gave England to his second son, who therefore became William II. However, he had a third son called Henry and I will tell you what happened to all of them next time you come here to see me."

A Norman soldier

CHAPTER 5

THE NORMANS Part 2

William II 1087-1100
Henry I 1100-1135 and Stephen 1135-1154

The very next day Sam and Nikki were again able to visit their grandparents... on their way they chatted to one another...

"...what do you think about the Normans, Sam?" asked Nikki.

"They seem to have been a rough sort of people to me," he replied.

"I wonder if Grandpa knows from where they came?"

"From Normandy, silly," said Sam.

"No, I mean before that," she said.

"Let's ask... look he's coming now," said Sam. "Grandpa, who were the Normans? I mean do you know where they came from in the first place?"

"Yes, I can tell you, but I think you may be able to guess. What does 'Nor-man' sound like?"

"North man perhaps?" replied Sam.

"Almost correct," replied his grandfather, "actually it comes from 'Norse-man'. People we have already mentioned in our story of England. Norsemen was another name for the Vikings. "

"Gosh," said Nikki, "so did the same people who settled in England, settle in France as well?"

"They did, and even before that, remember it was people from Roman Britain, who also settled in northern France, or Gaul, when the Saxons came."

"So does it mean that the descendants of the Vikings and Britons from France, which we now call Normans, were fighting the descendants of their own ancestors in England?" said Nikki.

"Quite right."

"Could they speak to each other in the same language then?" asked Sam.

"Some could, but not the uneducated ordinary people, I suspect," said his grandfather.

"I wonder if they knew they had common ancestors?"

"I don't expect so... but do you want me to continue the story of the Normans?"

"Yes, please," they both said.

"Please remind me where it was that we stopped yesterday."

"It was when William I died, and William II became king of England," said Sam.

"...and the eldest brother Robert became Duke of Normandy... and their other brother was Henry," added Nikki.

"What sort of a king was William II?" asked Sam.

"Well, it all depends whose side you are on," replied their grandfather.

"I think I'm on the side of the Anglo-Saxons," said Nikki.

"In that case, you would not have been very pleased with him, because he continued to act very harshly towards the local population, and even several of his father's nobles rebelled against him. The problem was, that under the feudal system most of the nobles had lands in Normandy and in England, and they owed their loyalty to two different people."

"You mean Robert and William II ?" said Sam.

"Yes, that's right."

" William eventually overcame his nobles, but he exiled from England one noble family called 'de Clare' for several years; they were among those who thought his elder brother Robert should be king.

Caerphilly Castle, a home of the de Clare family

The quarrels between William and Robert got worse, but eventually they did make a pact not to fight each other and agreed that whoever lived the longest would inherit the lands of the other... they also agreed that their youngest brother Henry should not inherit anything!"

"That seems a bit unkind," said Nikki.

"... and it had some serious consequences," continued her grandfather.

"Ooo... what happened Grandpa?" said Sam.

"I'm afraid it seems most likely that Henry and the de Clare family plotted to have William II killed, and organised an "accident" to happen to William whilst they were all out hunting in the New Forest in the year 1100. An arrow fired by one member of the hunting party, who was married to a daughter of the 'de Clare' family, killed the king. Whilst the killer escaped to France in a waiting boat, Henry galloped to Winchester where he got control of the treasury and persuaded the nobles to make him king. The place where William II died in the New Forest is today marked by a stone called 'The Rufus Stone'."

The Rufus Stone… in the New Forest

"Why 'Rufus' Grandpa?" asked Nikki.

"Rufus was William's nick-name… it means he had red hair or a red face."

"Are there any other things for which we should remember William Rufus?" asked Sam.

"Only one… he was the king that ordered the building in London of Westminster Hall in 1097, which was for many centuries the place where the kings or their representatives decided all important legal matters… it is still there today. It was rebuilt by King Richard II in 1394…have you ever been inside?"

"No, I don't think we have," said the children.

"I will take you there one day then," replied their grandfather, "because it has an important place in English history."

"What did they do with William II's body in the New Forest?" asked Sam.

"They got a local man to put it in a cart and he took it to Winchester, where it was buried in the cathedral."

"What did Robert think of Henry becoming King of England?" asked Nikki.

"Well, to start with Robert was away taking part in the First Crusade, so he didn't find out what had happened for a while, but..."

"Excuse me Grandpa," said Nikki, "what was the 'crusade'?"

"The crusade was a war that The Pope encouraged the European Christian kings and leaders to undertake, to win back the land where Jesus was born from the control of the Muslims."

"Oh, I see."

"Robert got back from the crusade [which was successful by the way] and he was very angry, so he invaded England to fight Henry in 1101. However at Alton in Hampshire, the brothers made a peace treaty, which allowed Henry to stay as king, but he had to pay his brother money every year. After a few years Henry decided he would invade Normandy and stop paying the money to Robert, and at a great battle he captured his brother, so he then gained control of both territories like his father William the Conqueror."

"Do you know what happened to Robert, Grandpa?" asked Sam.

"He was imprisoned by Henry in Cardiff Castle for 28 years until he died."

"What a family!" said Nikki. "I don't think I like Henry."

"Actually, although Henry I was not a very nice person perhaps, he turned out be quite a good ruler... he was a bit like his father in that

Cardiff Castle (rebuilt). The place of imprisonment of Robert, Duke of Normandy

he liked organisation and arranged for the fair collection of taxes and the proper management of justice. England was very peaceful during his reign, but it didn't last after his death I'm afraid."

"Why was that, Grandpa?" asked Nikki.

"Sadly his son and heir, named William, died in a shipwreck whilst returning to England from Normandy in the year 1120 and so when Henry himself died in 1135, there was a dispute between the rival claimants to his throne. Henry had hoped that the barons would accept his eldest daughter Mathilda, who was married to a French nobleman, the Count of Anjou, but most of them were not ready to have a woman in charge, and they preferred the grandson of William the Conqueror, named Stephen, and he was crowned king. The result was civil war, because Mathilda came to England to try to force Stephen from the throne."

"Not more wars!" exclaimed Nikki, "they never seem to stop."

"I'm afraid so; this one hardly stopped at all, and went on for nineteen years, and caused great hardship to the ordinary people of England. Unfortunately, Stephen was a weak king and could not control his barons, so when they weren't fighting either for him or against him, they were fighting each other."

"Grandpa," said Sam.

"Yes."

"It is interesting how England's story seems to depend on kings."

"Indeed it does, and particularly at this time in its history, because as I have told you the 'feudal system' was based entirely on the ownership of land. The king controlled the land and gave it to his barons and other friends, who in turn gave it to lesser nobles, who in turn gave it to the peasants; they were the ones who actually grew the crops and looked after the cattle, which created the only form of wealth. As the years passed, all these different classes also gave land to the church, so eventually the church became among the wealthiest of all sections of that society."

"How did the war between Stephen and Mathilda end, Grandpa?" said Nikki. "Did King Stephen die, or did Mathilda go back to France?"

King Stephen signs the Treaty of Winchester 1153

"Both of those things happened... however before that, Mathilda's son also called Henry, decided to invade England on his mother's behalf, and it was in Winchester in 1153 that Stephen, agreed that Henry should succeed him as king when he died and so the war finally ended. When King Stephen died the following year he was the last of the Normans."

"Gosh! Was that all there was to the Normans... they didn't last long then, did they Grandpa?" said Sam.

"The Norman kings may not have lasted very long but their influence on England was very great, for remember, they began the building of most of our castles and cathedrals, and in organising the country's finances they set their seal on much of England for the next 300 years, in what became known as 'The Middle Ages'. Don't forget also that although the new King Henry's family name was 'Plantagenet' and he became king as Henry II, he was actually the grandson of the Norman King Henry I.

"How old was Henry II when he became king?" asked Nikki.

"Just twenty-one," replied her grandfather, "and because of his marriage to Eleanor of Aquitaine he gained control of most of France and was suddenly the richest king in Europe... at the end of their lives they both chose to be buried in France. However, now I think this is a good place to stop for the moment; I can tell you more about Henry II and the rest of the 'Plantagenets' next time we meet."

"Thank you Grandpa."

"It's all very interesting."

Tombs of Henry II and Eleanor in Fontevraud Abbey in France

CHAPTER 6

THE FIRST PLANTAGENETS

Henry II 1154–1189 and Richard I 1189–1199

"Grandpa," said Nikki, when they next met, "does 'Plantagenet' have a meaning?"

"It does; I believe it began as a nickname for Henry's father, who was known to wear a sprig of broom in his helmet [plant-a-genet means plant-in-helmet]."

"Wasn't that a bit odd?" asked Sam.

"Not really, because you have to remember that when knights were dressed for battle it was almost impossible to tell one from another, so fixing something distinctive in your helmet might have been a very good idea, but no one is absolutely sure if that is the real origin of the name."

"Grandpa," said Nikki, "Last time I think you said Henry II was very rich and that he married a very rich French lady... was he a good king as well?"

"I think he was. He managed to restore all the good things done by Henry I, which had been forgotten during Stephen's reign and improved upon them. He was one of England's greatest kings, but there is one important story about him that I must tell you; it's the story of Henry's best friend who became his worst enemy!"

"Gosh, who was that Grandpa?" said Sam.

"Thomas-à-Becket, whom Henry made his Chancellor and then his Archbishop of Canterbury."

"Could he do both jobs then?" asked Sam.

"No ... and that was the problem. As soon as Thomas became Archbishop, he gave up being Chancellor and became very serious about his duties to the church and the Pope. Henry could not understand how his best friend could take sides against him on behalf of the church and their arguments became worse and worse. One day in 1170 when Henry was in France, in a fit of rage, he said to his courtiers that he wished someone would get rid of Thomas. Secretly, four of his knights decided to help the king and win his favour... they sailed to England and rode to Canterbury; when Thomas would not go with them they killed him in the Cathedral. The whole world was shocked by their terrible deed and Henry II wished he could have controlled himself better and was very sorry. The Pope decided that Henry should make amends and do a penance for instigating the murder of the archbishop."

"What's a 'penance' please Grandpa?" asked Sam.

"A penance is an act of saying sorry in a special way. Henry's penance was to wear sackcloth and ashes and to walk before his

Murder of Thomas a Becket in Canterbury Cathedral 1170

subjects to Canterbury Cathedral and to stay there all night praying for forgiveness in front of Thomas' tomb."

"Did the Pope and the people forgive him?" asked Nikki.

"Yes they did, and almost at once the Pope declared that Thomas would be a saint. Thereafter for more than 300 years people made pilgrimages to the shrine of St. Thomas in Canterbury in the hope of being cured of illnesses and to gain favour with God."

"Do people still go on pilgrimages today, Grandpa?" asked Sam.

"Yes they do. You may have heard of a place in France called Lourdes, to which people go as pilgrims and where some miracle cures have happened."

"I don't think I have," said Nikki thoughtfully, and then she said... "Grandpa, who came after Henry II?"

"It was his eldest son Richard, in 1189. There had been warlike disputes between Henry and his sons in the last years of his life, but it was a calm change of king this time."

"I think that Richard had another funny nickname," said Sam.

"You're thinking of 'Coeur de Lion'" replied his grandfather, "it means 'Heart of a Lion'... in other words, very brave."

"Was he a good or bad king?" asked Nikki.

"That is quite difficult to answer, because although he was very famous, he hardly spent any time in England during the ten years of his reign and he taxed the people very severely to finance his military exploits. As his nickname implies he was a brave soldier and even before becoming king he had decided to join a crusade to the 'Holy Land', thinking that his elder

The Pilgrim's Way… today

brother Geoffrey would succeed their father, but Geoffrey died in 1188 and his father one year later, and so to his surprise he became king."

"What happened on the crusade, and please, Grandpa, can you remind me of what it means?" asked Nikki, "I know you did tell us once before," she added.

"A crusade was a sort of religious war in The Holy Land [the part of the world where Israel is today], and I'm afraid to say this one was a bit of a disaster because Richard had arguments with both the other leaders, one of whom was the King of France and the other, the Duke of Austria, and they both left him in the Holy Land and went home. Next, Richard heard that his brother John was trying to become king in his place in England, so after some battles near Jerusalem a peace treaty was obtained with the Muslims. On his way home across Europe, Richard, disguised as a pilgrim, was captured by the duke he had offended and was imprisoned by him."

"Who looked after England while he was away, Grandpa?" asked Nikki.

"His mother Queen Eleanor and the chancellor, the Bishop of Ely. For a long while nobody knew what had happened to Richard. Eventually he was discovered [it is said] by his friend Blondel, a minstrel, who wandered around Europe looking for him. The Duke of Austria demanded a huge ransom for his safe return."

Durnstein Castle where King Richard was imprisoned

"How long was he in prison, Grandpa?" asked Sam.

"Just over a year, and his brother John and the King of France tried to bribe his Austrian captors to keep him there, but he was released in February 1194."

"Was he ever married?" asked Nikki.

"Yes, he was married in Cyprus to Princess Berengaria of Navarre in May 1191 on his way to the crusade, but they did not have any children."

"When did he die?" asked Sam.

"He died in 1199 whilst fighting in France. One day he was supervising the siege of a castle but not wearing his armour, and he was mortally wounded by an arrow"...

"... and then John became king?" continued Sam.

"He did."

"Now is it time for Magna Carta?" asked Nikki.

"Very nearly," replied her grandfather, "but Magna Carta was signed in 1215 and we're only at 1199, so there's a little way to go yet."

"Doesn't Robin Hood come into the story about this time?" asked Sam.

"Y...es, but I'm afraid Robin Hood is another 'King Arthur' figure."

"Do you mean 'true' but not all true?"

Robin Hood

Sherwood Forest... today

"Yes that's a good way to put it."

"Did he live in Sherwood Forest with his 'Merry Men'?"

"I believe so and the stories about him must be based on real events, but I expect that over the years they have been exaggerated. Whether there really was a very tall man called 'Little John' or another called 'Allan-a-dale...'"

"Or Will Scarlett?" asked Sam.

"...Or Friar Tuck?" said Nikki.

"Yes, yes, I can hear you know as much or more about Robin Hood than I do," said their grandfather. Of course his real 'claim to fame' was that he robbed the rich and gave to the poor, which was bound to be popular. Most of his supposed victims were high ranking church persons, abbots and bishops, and the wealth of these people was a great offence to the ordinary people, so he would have had a lot of support."

"Do you think he met King Richard, Grandpa, like in the film?" asked Nikki.

"I rather doubt it, but I'm sure there must be something true about his conflict with the Sheriff of Nottingham, and it would be nice to think that he married Maid Marian, wouldn't it?"

"Oh yes... anyway, we believe it don't we Sam?" said Nikki.

"Yes, and I've seen the stories about him on TV," said Sam,

"I'm afraid that is not real history... and I'm sure you know that," added his grandfather.

"Yes, I do realise that, but I do like the programmes," replied Sam then he added, "you know the sheriffs in the cowboy films Grandpa, is that where the name comes from?"

"Yes it is the same word, but of course in the olden times it meant something slightly different. Sheriff comes from 'shire reeve'; the reeve was the person who collected taxes for the king; every county or 'shire' [like Hamp-shire] had one or more shire-reeves or sheriffs as they came to be known... and there I think I'm going to stop today, because after Richard comes King John and the time of Magna Carta... a very important part of England's Story."

"Do we <u>have</u> to stop, Grandpa?" said Nikki.

"Yes, we've done enough for today and I've got to take Granny shopping. Will you see what you can find out about Magna Carta for me? We'll talk about that next time."

"Please, how do you spell it, Grandpa?" asked Nikki.

"M*A*G*N*A, C*A*R*T*A."

"Thank you. I'll do my best."

"So will I," said Sam.

Magna Carta Memorial, Runnymede

CHAPTER 7

THE PLANTAGENETS Part 2

King John 1199–1216
Henry III 1216–1272
Edward I 1272–1307 and Edward II 1307–1327

This time it was a fortnight before the children met their grandfather again, and as on previous occasions it was not long before they settled down with him to listen to another episode of 'England's Story'.

"Grandpa."

"Yes."

"You know that you asked us to find out something about Magna Carta?"

"Yes."

"Well Granny said that there's one of the original copies in Salisbury Cathedral."

"I'm sure that's right... did you find out anything else?"

"It was a document signed by King John in a meadow by the River Thames called 'Runnymede'," said Sam.

"You've both done very well, but you'll have to remind me where we finished last time."

"King Richard had just been killed and so John had just become king," said Nikki.

"Ah, yes... and he was a very unpopular king too."

"Why was that Grandpa?" asked Nikki.

"Because he used the good laws made by his father Henry II, in a bad way and rather like his elder brother, he taxed the people very harshly to finance various wars in France, during which he lost most of his inherited possessions there. Luckily for England the Pope appointed a very good man called Stephen Langton, to be Archbishop of Canterbury and he tried his best to keep the peace between the people, the barons and the king. However for five years John would not accept Stephen Langton and there was a big fuss and the Pope placed an 'interdict' on the whole of England."

"Excuse me Grandpa, what's an interdict?" asked Sam.

Runnymede, by the River Thames, where Magna Carta was signed in 1215

"A prohibition by the pope to all priests in a country to stop them performing all church services."

"Goodness, does that mean no one could be buried, and things?" asked Sam.

"No burials, no marriages, no baptisms for five years."

"No wonder the people did not like King John," said Nikki.

"Eventually, the barons could not accept John's actions and with Archbishop Langton's help, the Great Charter, or Magna Carta, was drawn up and signed at Runnymede to try to establish once and for all the rule of law."

"Where did they get the idea?" asked Sam.

"The archbishop remembered the 'charter', in which Henry I had given his word to the barons about their rights and responsibilities almost 100 years before. He hoped by making a new one, a civil war in England would be prevented."

"Did he succeed?"

"Up to a point he did, but a war did start, during which John became ill and died."

"What happened then, Grandpa?"

"Well there was no more reason for a war and King John's son Henry, became King Henry III at the age of nine and he remained king for the next 56 years."

"Where was he crowned," asked Sam.

"In Gloucester Cathedral, and 'crowned' is not the right expression in his case, because his father had lost all the crown jewels shortly before

King John's baggage (including the Crown Jewels) lost crossing The Wash

he died, when the cart they were being carried in, sank in a muddy river in East Anglia, so all they could do for the new boy-king, was to make a small circlet of gold to place on his head during the ceremony."

"Was his reign peaceful?" asked Nikki.

"Thankfully for the start it was... he had some very good advisers, who really did all the work for him, particularly Archbishop Stephen Langton and a nobleman called Hubert de Burgh. Both of them felt very deeply for the rights of Englishmen in general and in 1225 they revised and re-issued the Magna Carta in its final form in the name of the new king."

"That was a good thing, I suppose," said Sam.

"Yes it was because it became the foundation of our laws. I'm afraid peace and quiet did not last long however, because in 1229 when the king was 22 he decided to take the powers of government himself and appointed people from his French possessions to positions of power, which annoyed the English nobles. Next he married a French princess and gave her relations high offices of state... one I must mention was named Simon de Montfort."

"Why Grandpa?"

"He was a very clever person as a soldier and an administrator and even married the king's sister. Later in the king's reign when Henry had behaved badly, he took sides with the ordinary Englishmen against the king and won the Battle of Lewes in Sussex, capturing both the king and his son Edward."

"Did he try to become king himself?" asked Sam.

"No, he was very careful not to take away the king's power but tried to use it wisely on his behalf and was very respectful to Prince Edward. In order to gain some extra authority to his ruling the country, he ordered representatives to come to London from all the boroughs and counties for a 'parlement'."

"Parliament!" said Sam, "Is that when it began? What date was that Grandpa?"

"1265... it's a date to remember!"

"What did the king think about it?" asked Nikki.

"Like his father King John, he could not abide having his royal power subject to the views of ordinary people, but since he was a captive of Simon, there was little he could do about it."

"How did it all end Grandpa?"

"Actually Prince Edward escaped and decided to rescue his father from Simon and a battle was fought at Evesham at the end of 1265 and Simon was killed... but his ideas did not die and after Henry III died in 1272, and Edward became King Edward I, he remembered the good things Simon had introduced and built upon them."

"Apart from giving positions of power to his French relations, did Henry do anything else for us to remember?" asked Nikki.

"Yes, he did. Henry was quite a religious man and I'm sure he would like to be remembered for rebuilding Westminster Abbey in London. He spent a vast fortune of his own money on the project and it remains today very

Salisbury Cathedral… where one of the original copies of MAGNA CARTA is kept

much as he wanted it to be. He is buried there close to the tomb of the abbey's first builder, Edward the Confessor. Another famous cathedral was built during his reign, and that was Salisbury."

"Can we go there one day?" said Nikki.

"... and see their copy of Magna Carta?" continued Sam.

"I don't see why not," replied their grandfather... " it is a very historic city and there's lots to see as well as the cathedral. We could even start our outing at Old Sarum where the first cathedral was built."

"That's a funny name," said Nikki giggling, "it sounds like 'old Sarah'!"

"I suppose it does; but actually it is an old hill-fort from long before the Roman times with several huge earth walls built around the top of a hill. Both the Romans and the Normans used it as a base and there was a town inside... Sarum is the name the Romans called it."

Old Sarum, with Salisbury in the distance

"Is there time for you to tell us about Edward I?" asked Sam.

"I think so. Edward was thirty-three years old and a very well-known soldier in Europe. Apparently, he was in Sicily when he heard the news of his father's death and yet he didn't return to England for two years."

"How strange," said Nikki, "he must have been very confident of his position."

"Yes, I imagine the fact that he was the only son of his father had something to do with it," said her grandfather.

"Was he a good king?" asked Sam.

"I think I would say he was, because as I have already told you, he developed the idea of Simon de Montfort's parliaments and ordered them to meet regularly every May and September ... one of his expressions is reputed to have been, 'that which touches all, should be approved by all'."

We would say 'affects all' instead of 'touches all' today I think. He understood that a king could rule much better with the support of his chief subjects. He was a clever man and always wanted to solve difficulties by the use of laws rather than fighting if he could. He longed to be able to give the rule of law to the whole of Britain. Part of his 'grand plan' was to add Wales to his domains. You will remember that the Romans never conquered Wales and when the Saxons came, even more of the original British people retreated into Wales; the Normans likewise never conquered Wales, so it had really been a place from which there was always raiding parties into England, or vice versa."

"Excuse me Grandpa, but what does 'vice versa' mean?"

"It means 'the other way round... the English raided into Wales'.

"Oh, thank you."

"Was Edward successful in his plan for Wales?" asked Sam.

"Yes he was. He tried to use his idea of law to achieve his aim, but when the Welsh ignored their treaty with him, he invaded their territory with a great army and Wales became part of England in 1284...to consolidate his power in that country he built some of the most impressive castles ever seen. His son, Edward, who later became the next king, was born in Caernarvon Castle in the same year. Later, he was given the title of Prince of Wales, and from that day to this, the eldest son of the monarch is given the same title, as I'm sure you know."

"Grandpa, said Sam.

"Yes."

"You said that Edward wanted to give English laws to the whole of Britain, so did he next go to Scotland?"

Caernarvon Castle, North Wales… Built by Edward I

"He certainly did. In fact he was invited by the Scots to help them decide who should be their next king when the Scottish throne became vacant in 1291. The man he chose later rebelled against him and Edward took his revenge by defeating him in a battle at Dunbar in 1296. There were almost continual conflicts with the Scots during the next years, and it was on his way to fight in Scotland again in 1307 that Edward died at Burgh-by-Sands, a place near the western end of Hadrian's Wall."

"What should we most remember about him do you think Grandpa?" asked Sam.

"I think I would say... for his ideas about the use of law and the encouragement of parliaments."

"I'm going to remember him for his castles in Wales," said Nikki. "Perhaps one day we can go and see some of them," she added.

"Wales is indeed a lovely country to visit and not only for its castles; don't forget that in North Wales there is one of our highest mountains, called Mount Snowdon, and there is a railway line right to the top!"

"Wow, that's cool!" said Sam... then he added, "Can we hear about the next king before we go home please Grandpa?"

"Yes, there is time, but I'm sorry to have to tell you England suffered greatly under the new weak king, Edward II."

"Oh, dear," said Nikki, "more trouble then... was Edward II a baby?"

"No, he was twenty-three years old but by his choice of friends and advisers and his general behaviour [rather like his grandfather]; he managed to upset just about everyone. His father had wanted him to continue the war against the Scots, but he wasn't really interested. The Scots realised this and under the command of Robert the Bruce they began to invade England and to do much damage. Eventually Edward decided he had to do something about them and he assembled a vast army. A battle was fought between them near the town of Stirling, at a place called Bannockburn in 1314 and the English were soundly defeated."

Stirling Castle... today

"Was Edward captured?" asked Sam.

"No, he escaped, but things went from bad to worse… his barons and even his own queen eventually rebelled against him. In 1325 the queen went to France and persuaded her husband to send over to her their son [also called Edward]. In France she arranged her son's marriage and then returned with him and some troops and captured her husband. A parliament was called, which under her influence deposed Edward II, forcing him to abdicate in favour of his son, who became Edward III. Do you know what abdicate means?"

"Does it mean 'give up the throne'?"

"Yes that's right. Since Edward III was only fifteen, it meant that his mother the Queen and her best friend the Earl of March, then ruled the country."

"What became of Edward II, Grandpa?" asked Nikki.

"I'm afraid he was cruelly murdered in Berkeley Castle in Gloucestershire, probably on the orders of the Earl of March in 1327… and that's where we must stop for today. The next reign, of Edward III, is a very important one in our story and I will have to do some homework before we meet again. If you like you can do some too… do your best to find out about two things, 'The Black Death' and 'The Black Prince'… who wants to do the first?"

"I'll do 'The Black Death'", said Sam.

"So that leaves you with 'The Black Prince' Nikki… is that OK?"

"Yes Grandpa, but I'm not sure where to start looking."

"I'm sure your parents will help you both," replied their grandfather, "and of course there's always your computer."

Berkeley Castle …today

46

CHAPTER 8

THE PLANTAGENETS Part 3

Edward III 1327–1377
Richard II 1377–1399 and Henry IV 1399–1413

A few days later Nikki and Sam were talking to each other about their finding out things for their grandfather.

"What did you find out about 'The Black Death', Sam?" asked Nikki.

"It was a disease that came to England from Europe in 1348, and lots and lots of people died... hundreds of thousands! In some villages and towns only about a third of people survived."

"Did you find out what caused it?" she asked,

"I think it was the bites from fleas on infected rats."

"How horrible!" said Nikki.

"Did you find out about 'The Black Prince?" asked her brother.

"A little," said Nikki, "he was called The Black Prince because he wore black armour; and he was the eldest son of King Edward III."

"Grandpa said that he was an important king to know about," said Sam, "I wonder why?"

"Lots of reasons I expect," said Nikki, "anyway we'll soon find out because mum says that Grandpa is coming to our house this afternoon and we can ask him."

"The Black Prince sounds quite interesting."

"We will soon know!"

"Hello you two," said their grandfather, as they met later the same day, "how did you get on with the two questions?"

"O.K., I think," said Sam.

"Me too," said Nikki.

"Good, well done... I'll ask you about them when I come to the right part of the story in the reign of Edward III."

Sam said, "He was the son of Edward II... the one who was murdered, wasn't he?"

"Yes that's right. Just let me remind you that he became king at the age of fifteen, but to start with it was his mother and her friend the Earl of March, who ruled the country on his behalf."

"Do you think he minded, Grandpa?" asked Nikki.

"I rather think he did, because once he became eighteen he made a daring plan to take control himself. He helped some friends to enter Nottingham Castle by a secret passage late one evening, and arrested his mother and the Earl of March. You must remember that they had both been involved with his father's murder. The Earl he put to death and his mother he locked up in a nunnery for the rest of her life. He was a brave young man and quickly resolved to try to regain all his great grandfather's lands in France."

"Was his great-grandfather Henry III?"

"Yes that's correct. However, the French king would not agree to his claims and so Edward decided to attempt to regain them by force... and so began the 'Hundred Years War' between the two countries."

"A hundred years war!" exclaimed Nikki. "That's amazing; do you mean that the war went on for a hundred years?"

"Exactly... on and off for one hundred years."

"Who won?" asked Sam.

"Nobody really; generally speaking the English were the most successful in all the major battles and if Henry V had not died at the wrong moment in 1422, he would have been king of both countries... but we're getting too far ahead of ourselves, we must concentrate on Edward III."

"It sounds a pretty exciting time to me," said Sam.

"It was. Edward III had an amazing vision of himself as being a re-incarnation of King Arthur. Remembering the story of 'The Round Table', he saw himself as the leader of a select group of knights, the headquarters of which would be Windsor Castle.

Windsor Castle

48

Starting in 1350, he built the 'round tower' there and had another special building constructed to house a round table for himself and his knights. He had already instituted [in 1347] a new Order of Chivalry called 'The Order of The Garter', which still exists today and still the 'Knights of the Garter' are chosen only by the monarch."

Badge of the Order of the Garter

"Did they have tournaments and things?" asked Sam.

"Lots of them, and they were really practices for war, but there was a more important weapon that the English had when it came to actual fighting."

"Ooo, what was that, Grandpa?" asked Nikki.

"The 'longbow'... with it, the English archers became the most important men in the whole army. It was mostly their skill and the 'fire-power' of their bows that won the famous battles, even though they were always outnumbered by the French armies."

"What battles were those?" asked Sam.

"There were three main ones, the first was the Battle of Crecy in 1346, after which Edward became famous throughout Europe. His son also fought there in the English army; he was aged just sixteen, and his nickname, Nikki was...

"The Black Prince, Grandpa," she replied.

"Excellent. From this time onwards," continued their grandfather, "the military campaigns of Edward and his son in France were crowned with almost constant success... up to now the armoured knights had been the most important people on any battlefield, but after the Battle of Crecy no troops could withstand the immense power and range of the arrows fired by the longbows of the English archers. The next main battle that the English army won, at Poiters in 1356, was commanded by The Black Prince; even the French king himself was captured. However, before we reach that event something else happened to change the course of history in 1348, and that Sam, was..."

"The Black Death, Grandpa?"

"Quite right. So, what did you discover about it?"

"It was a terrible plague that affected every European country and lots and lots of people died very suddenly and at the time, no one knew how it was spread from one person to another."

"...Excuse me, did the war stop because of the plague, Grand-pa?" asked Nikki.

Longbow archers

"It did for a few years, but it had a more lasting effect on people's lives in other ways. After the Black Death there were insufficient people to grow the crops and look after the cattle and so the way in which the peasants were treated changed forever."

"In what way Grandpa?"

"The landowners found that they had to pay people to work for them.

From this time onwards the idea that peasants would work for nothing could not be sustained. Attempts by the government to return to the old ways, eventually led to 'the Peasants Revolt' in 1381... but more about that in a minute, again we must go back a bit, to continue the story of Edward III."

"What else did Edward III do, Grandpa?" asked Sam.

"Firstly, he realised that if he was to be successful in regaining his property in France, he would need safe communications across the English Channel, so he spent quite a lot of money building fighting ships and his navy won two important sea battles against the French during his reign. Secondly, in 1362 he ordered that the English language [not French] should be used in parliament and the courts."

"What happened to The Black Prince?" asked Nikki.

"In 1363 he was given the responsibility to rule the English lands in France. It was a difficult task and often he was away fighting in Spain as well. In later years all the lands that he and his father had gained there, were slowly won back by the French. The Black Prince returned to England in 1371 and died one year before his father in 1376... so he never became king. His tomb is in Canterbury Cathedral; I must take you to see it one day."

"If Edward III died in 1377," said Sam, "that means he ruled England for fifty years... how did he die?"

"I suppose you could say he died of 'old age'; sadly, he was gradually neglected by all his friends and family in spite of all his achievements and fame in war. However, it was because of his wars and therefore his

Tomb of the Black Prince in Canterbury Cathedral

constant needs for money, that our parliament became more and more important in England's story, for it developed into two 'houses' or gatherings... one for the 'Lords' and one for the 'Commons'... the names we still use today."

"Since The Black Prince died before his father, who became the next king?" asked Nikki.

"It was Richard, the son of the Black Prince. He became King Richard II at the age of ten."

"Another very young king," said Sam, " I suppose once again he needed help from adults to rule in his name."

"Yes, that's quite right; it was his uncle John of Gaunt who became head of the Council of Regency. They tried a new way to raise money to continue the war in France, by having a 'Poll Tax' [everyone had to pay the same regardless of how rich or poor they were]."

"That sounds very unfair," said Nikki.

"It was, and in 1381 [as I have already mentioned] there was the 'Peasants Revolt', which was very serious indeed while it lasted."

"What happened, Grandpa?" asked Sam.

"All over the country, but especially in Kent and Essex, the peasants

51

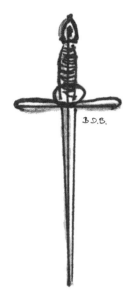

Sir William Walworth's dagger [40x17 cms] This killed Wat Tyler in 1381

defied the collectors of the Poll Tax and some collectors were killed. Within a few days thousands of the peasants marched to London, where the gates were opened to them by sympathisers inside the city. John of Gaunt's palace was burnt down and they even got inside The Tower and beheaded the Archbishop of Canterbury, who was the chancellor, or chief tax collector. The nobles did not know what to do, but the young king accompanied by the Lord Mayor of London agreed to meet the peasants outside the city. During the meeting the leader of the rebels, Wat Tyler, was killed whilst arguing with the King's advisers... this could have been very dangerous, but the fourteen year old King bravely rode towards the peasants and told them he would be their new leader and try to correct the injustices of which they were complaining, if they would go home peacefully... and they did."

"What happened to the people who had killed the tax collectors?" asked Nikki.

"They were arrested and put on trial; over the whole country about 150 were executed, but at the beginning of the next year the king proclaimed an amnesty for all the rest."

"What is an amnesty, please Grandpa?" asked Sam.

"It is a complete pardon for any previous wrong-doing."

"So the king was quite kind then," said Nikki.

"Yes he was; he was a young man with many good qualities, unfortunately he picked the wrong sort of friends and gave them great riches and important positions, which caused a lot of trouble with the nobles who were actually running the country for him. Another dispute with the nobles was that they wanted to re-start the war with France, and the king did not agree. Eventually the differences between the two groups broke out into civil war and the king's friends were defeated and executed."

"Was the king in any danger?" asked Sam.

"Yes he was, but one of the group of people against him was his cousin, Henry Bolingbroke, the son of John of Gaunt, and he saved him from any harm. King Richard however, never forgot who was responsible for killing his friends and in later years took his revenge against them. The next year, 1389, Richard [now twenty-two] informed the Council of Regency

Westminster Hall re-roofed in 1394

that he was going to take full charge of the government and he spent money very lavishly."

"What on, Grandpa?"

"On his palaces mostly and their furnishings and fitments... he was probably the first person to have hot and cold running water in his bathroom since the Roman times! To his credit he also rebuilt Westminster Hall and had a wonderful new wooden roof put on it."

"Is it still there?"

"Yes it is... as I've already promised you, that's another place for us to visit some day. It forms part of what we call today 'The Houses of Parliament'. For the next few years there was peace in England, but in 1394 Richard's queen, called Anne of Bohemia, died, and she had been a good influence upon him. After her death Richard began to govern more and more like a dictator. In 1398 he even banished his cousin, Henry Bolingbroke, who had saved his life. Then in February 1399 his uncle John of Gaunt died and very foolishly he decided to confiscate all his cousin Henry's inherited estates."

53

"I bet that made Henry very angry," said Nikki.

"It did, and most of the other important people also realised that they too could be given the same treatment and perhaps have all their lands confiscated if they died, so suddenly there was a lot of secret opposition to Richard. In May 1399 Richard decided to go to Ireland; as soon as Henry heard about it he left France and sailed back to England to claim his estates, by force if necessary. Soon Henry had an army and although Richard came back from Ireland to fight him, he soon surrendered to Henry. With Richard in his power, by the will of parliament, Henry was crowned King Henry IV in October 1399. Richard died in prison in Pontefract Castle but nobody quite knows how it happened."

Pontefract Castle (demolished 1650)

"Was he murdered like Edward II?" asked Nikki.

"Maybe ... no one knows; and from time to time during Henry IV's reign it was rumoured that he was still alive, but his death is accepted as being in 1400."

"What do you think it is best for us to remember about Richard II, Grandpa?" asked Nikki.

"I think he should be given credit for his leadership during the Peasants Revolt being such a young age at the time, but his style of government was not suited to the English people in general, and he became very dictatorial and vindictive."

54

"Excuse me Grandpa but what does vindictive mean?" asked Sam.
"Revengeful."

"What about Henry IV? Did he have an easy time as king?" asked Nikki.

"No... I think Shakespeare in his play called 'Henry IV' has the line, 'uneasy lies the head that wears the crown'. I think he did his best and was quite popular with most ordinary people, but there were frequent plots against him. The one thing he did, **and had to do**, was to restore the status of parliament because his authority rested upon their approval."

"Did he go to war against France? You said there were three main battles in the Hundred Years War and you've only talked about two of them," said Sam.

"We shall get to the third battle quite soon but not during Henry IV's reign. Fighting in France was one thing he <u>did</u> avoid. The thirty year truce signed in 1396 by Richard II remained in force. Actually he had enough problems fighting the Welsh, the Scots and some of his former supporters like the Earl of Northumberland, whose son, nicknamed 'Hotspur' was killed at the Battle of Shrewsbury only four years after he became king."

Alnwick Castle, home of the Earls and Dukes of Northumberland

"Northumberland is near Scotland isn't it?" said Nikki.

"Yes, the Earls of Northumberland were always very important in protecting England from the Scots. Henry pardoned the earl for his son's rebellion, but in 1405 the Earl rebelled again."

"What happened this time, Grandpa?" asked Sam.

"Henry again defeated the rebels, and this time all the leaders had

55

their heads chopped off... except for the Earl himself, who escaped to Scotland and stayed there. It was about this time that Henry started to become ill; by 1411 he was so ill that his son [soon to be the next king anyway], tried to persuade his father to give up the crown to him. However Henry IV having usurped the crown from his cousin Richard II, would not let his son do the same to him!"

"What does 'usurped' mean please Grandpa?" asked Nikki.

"To take possession of power, illegally, by force."

"Oh, thank you."

"When did Henry IV finally die?" asked Sam.

"In March 1413. A rather sad end for a man who I think, wanted to do the best for his country, but never felt secure in his position as its king."

"Was the Hundred Years War finished yet Grandpa?"

"No, not yet, and during the reign of our next king, Henry V, we come to the third great battle when it seemed that England had finally won the victory, but..."

"... but what, Grandpa?"

"... but, you'll have to wait for our next time together to find out I'm afraid."

"Oh, Grandpa that's not fair; I wish we could know now," said Sam.

"The next part of our story is well worth waiting for, I can tell you," replied their grandfather.

"What about finding out about something again for next time?" asked Nikki.

"O.K., you can both do the same subject... how about the third great battle which became one of the greatest victories in England's history, the Battle of Agincourt? I would like each of you to find out something about that, if you can."

CHAPTER 9

THE PLANTAGENETS Part 4

Henry V 1413–1422
Henry VI 1422–1461
Edward IV 1461–1483
Edward V 1483 and Richard III 1483–1485

B.D.B

Some time passed before the twins Nikki and Sam were with their grandfather again, then one day their mother had a telephone call from him asking if the children would like to come over to tea the following day. Both said 'yes' and when the next day came they all found themselves sitting in comfortable chairs in the shade of a silver birch tree in their grandparents garden... their grandmother said, "I'm just going into the kitchen to prepare our tea, so now would be a good time for Grandpa to continue his story for you. Did you manage to find out about the Battle of Agincourt?"

B.D.B.
Under the Silver Birch tree

"I found out that Agincourt was in northern France," said Nikki.

"... and I found out that it was fought on 25th October 1415," said Sam.

"Well that's a good start; now I'll leave you to your grandfather to tell you about Henry V, who won the battle."

"Thank you, I'll do my best," he said.

"Excuse me Grandpa," said Nikki, "but how old was Henry V when he became king?"

"Twenty-five years old. First of all he declared an amnesty. Do you both remember what that means?"

"Yes, Grandpa," they both said.

"He very soon realised that the parliament and the nobles wanted to re-start the' Hundred Years War' with France [and he liked the idea too], so he started up the old quarrel with that country again and set about organising an invasion force."

"Do you know how many men he had in his army Grandpa?" asked Sam.

"About 10,000...they were a mixture of archers and armoured knights."

"Did it take long to get them all together?" asked Nikki.

"I don't know if you would call it long... I suppose it did, but the preparations for such an important expedition took over a year, and included making an alliance with the Duke of Burgundy, before they all set sail from Southampton in August 1415."

"What happened when they arrived in France?"

"First of all they besieged the town of Harfleur; this took a long time to capture and so many of his soldiers became sick or died that Henry V was advised to return to England with the 5000 that remained. He therefore set off to march to Calais to meet his ships. The French heard about his lack of men and decided to block his route. On 25th October at Agincourt the two armies faced each other [5000 English against 20,000 French]. As at Crecy and Poitiers long before, it was the power of the English archers that decided the outcome... in the space of two or three hours the French forces were utterly defeated."

"Wow! That was amazing," said Sam.

"It certainly was. Henry arrived back in England to a 'hero's welcome'. More expeditions went to France in the next few years and were also successful; by the Treaty of Troyes in 1420, it was agreed that Henry would marry the daughter of the French king and that when the French king died, Henry would become king of both countries."

"So was it all over really? Was it complete victory for England?" asked Sam.

"I'm afraid not, history is never quite as simple as that, for even though Henry was, as we say 'in the prime of life', in 1422 he suddenly died."

"So he never became King of France as well as England," said Nikki.

"No he did not."

"Who succeeded him Grandpa?" asked Nikki.

"It was his nine months old baby son and he became Henry VI. Two months later when the French king died

St Joan of Arc

58

this little baby became King of France and England. He was actually crowned in Paris in 1431."

"I think this is going to be the same story that we've heard before," said Nikki, "a young king needing other people to rule for him."

"Yes, it was his father's brothers, the Dukes of Bedford and Gloucester that controlled the government for him. Of course it was not realised until he began to grow up that he had an inherited illness of his mind, and although he was supposedly king for fifty years, really he always required guidance. He was pious and kind but these qualities were always overshadowed by his incompetence and feebleness of mind."

"Didn't people help him Grandpa?" asked Nikki.

"Yes, some did try, but his uncles and later his wife really controlled him. To have a weak king just at this time was a disaster for both countries, and to add to the problems in France, the French found an unlikely military leader; a young lady called Joan of Arc, who suddenly inspired them to regain their lands from the English and to win many battles against them."

"What happened to her Grandpa?"

"Eventually, she was captured and to our country's great shame, she was burnt to death in Rouen in May 1431; not because of her military exploits against us, but because it was deemed that she had offended the church."

St Joan of Arc being burnt at the stake in Rouen

"Oh dear! How sad."

"The Duke of Bedford, who was the king's representative in France, died four years later in 1435, and thereafter the English once again gradually lost all their possessions in that country, so that by the year 1453 the only town England still controlled, was Calais."

"Why did that happen Grandpa?" asked Sam.

"It was chiefly due to lack of good leadership, and also because the French made the best use of a new weapon... gunpowder. The old walled cities and castles could no longer be defended against that sort of attack... but I'm going a bit too far ahead. I must just tell you that in 1437, when his mother died, the sixteen years old King Henry VI assumed 'royal power'; whereupon his only remaining uncle, the Duke of Gloucester retired and devoted his energies to creating a library for the University of Oxford. The King's new chief adviser was another family friend of the king, the Duke of Suffolk, and 1445 he, with the help of the King of France, arranged a marriage for Henry VI with Margaret of Anjou. The marriage treaty contained a secret clause that England would give to France the province of Maine."

"Could a duke just do that, without telling anyone?" asked Nikki.

"No, it was a very dangerous thing to do and in the end [when it became known] the duke lost his life because of it," replied her grandfather." In the mean time the king's uncle the Duke of Gloucester died in suspicious circumstances whilst attending a parliament called by the Duke of Suffolk on behalf of the king. It was because of the deaths of these two dukes [Gloucester and later, Suffolk] that gradually a new civil war began in England, called the Wars of the Roses."

"Why the 'Roses', Grandpa?" asked Sam.

Red Rose

"Because the two sides, of what was really a family dispute, adopted 'roses' for the badges of their soldiers... a red rose for the Lancastrians and a white rose for their opponents, the Yorkists."

"It must have been an important family," said Sam.

"It was... it was the 'royal family'.

White Rose

Both families were descended from sons of Edward III; one was descended from John of Gaunt, Duke of Lancaster and the other from Edmund, Duke of York. Of course both of those brothers had died years before this. However, because things in general in both England and France were going so badly under Henry VI, the sons and grandsons of these two began to fight for power in England."

"How long did the Wars of the Roses last?" asked Nikki.

"Oh, it went on for at least thirty years, I think."

"How did it end?" asked Sam.

"I suppose it could be said that during the time of this war so many leaders on both sides either died or were executed by their foes, that there was almost nobody left to carry it on! However, before we get to that point in our story, we have to get to know at least three more kings."

"Who were they Grandpa?"

"Edward IV, Edward V and Richard III [all belonged to the Yorkist family], and we shall soon come to the first of them, but I'm sure you must be wondering what happened to poor old Henry VI. By the year 1450 Henry VI was so ill that he could not govern the country; Richard, Duke of York, was seen by most to be a good alternative and in fact when the king got worse in 1453 he officially became 'Protector'... then a year later the king got better."

"Then what happened?" asked Sam.

"I'm afraid this was when the civil war, called The Wars of the Roses, started ... first one side won and then the other until it seemed the Yorkists were at last triumphant at the Battle of Towton, near York, in 1461. After this battle Henry VI escaped and was hidden away somewhere and because Richard, Duke of York had been killed the previous year, his son, Edward, proclaimed himself King Edward IV."

"So now there were two kings!" said Sam.

"Yes. Eventually, three years later Henry was discovered; taken to London and imprisoned in The Tower; in the mean time, Edward IV did his best to make friends with his Lancastrian enemies, but they turned against him... thereafter he was ruthless in killing them whenever possible. A few years went by fairly peacefully and then in 1470 Edward's close friend the Earl of Warwick suddenly changed sides and captured Edward IV and decided that he would make Henry VI king again."

"Goodness, what a change for Henry!" said Nikki.

"Why do you think it was that Edward didn't kill Henry when he had him in his power?" asked Sam.

"I expect it was because Henry's queen, Margaret, and her son the Prince of Wales were safely in France and it suited Edward better at least to have Henry under his control rather than dead, because then Henry's son would officially become the rightful new king against him."

Eton College founded by Henry VI

61

"... and then what happened Grandpa?" asked Nikki.

"There was a year or so when it seemed that nobody could trust anyone at all, they continually double-crossed each other, and all of them at different times had to escape to safety in France, even Edward himself. However, in May 1471 Edward returned to England and finally defeated his former friend the Earl of Warwick at the Battle of Barnet, near London, and a month later he defeated Queen Margaret at the Battle of Tewkesbury, where her son the Prince of Wales was killed. Now at last there was no further need to keep Henry VI alive, and he was murdered in The Tower of London, probably on the orders of Edward's brother, Richard the Duke of Gloucester."

"Poor Henry VI," said Nikki, "he didn't have much of a life did he?"

"No, his whole fifty years was affected by the ambitions of his relatives, but he deserves his place in history in spite of his feebleness of mind for his piety and his great educational projects. In 1441 he decided to have a school built at Eton and a college at Cambridge University, called 'Kings College'...I'm sure you have heard of them, both were very important in England's Story, and still are today."

"With Henry VI now dead," said Sam, "was that the end of the Wars of the Roses?"

"Not quite... there's a little bit more to come, Edward IV continued to reign until his own death in 1483 at the age of forty."

"Did he have any children?" asked Nikki.

King's College Chapel, Cambridge …today

"Yes, he had married a lady by the name of Elizabeth Woodville in 1464 and they had three children, Elizabeth, Edward and Richard, and I will tell you about their stories too. You ought also to remember him as the king who permitted William Caxton to set up the very first printing press in England, near Westminster Abbey, in 1476."

William Caxton's printing press at Westminster Abbey

"Grandpa didn't give us anything to find out," said Nikki talking to her brother Sam when they were on their own again, "can you remember what comes next?"

"I expect it's Edward V after Edward IV, don't you?"

"I suppose so, but Grandpa said that all <u>three</u> of Edward IV's children come into our story."

"I bet it's something to do with having a young boy as king again," said Nikki.

"We'll find out tomorrow," said Sam.

"Grandpa, is it going to be Edward V after Edward IV?" asked Sam the following day.

"It is, but only just... and I'm afraid I can't spend very long with you today!"

"Never mind Grandpa."

Nikki turned to Sam, "What did I tell you," she said. "I think it's going to be 'uncle trouble' again."

"Quite right, and I'm afraid it's a terrible story. When Edward IV died he had only one brother still living, Richard, Duke of Gloucester, it was natural therefore that he should become 'guardian' to the young boy Edward V. Using the excuse that he needed to protect Edward V and his brother Richard, he had them both placed in The Tower of London...they never saw their mother or sister ever again."

"Gosh, what happened?" asked Nikki.

"I'm afraid that Richard's own ambition got the better of him; he arranged to have the two princes murdered and then proclaimed himself King Richard III."

"What a cruel man!" said Nikki.

"They were cruel times... it did not do him any good; his guilt played on his mind forever afterwards and before long people were demanding that the princes should be set free... when they couldn't be, people drew their own conclusions that they were dead and Richard III became a feared and hated man."

"I'm not surprised," said Sam, "did he last long as king?"

"No. Richard III was the last of the Yorkist leaders and there was another person who was the last of the Lancastrians called Henry Tudor, Earl of Richmond. Henry invaded England from France in 1485 and defeated Richard at the Battle of Bosworth. Richard was killed and Henry became the new king, Henry VII. He sensibly and quickly married Elizabeth of York, the elder sister of the murdered princes, and finally the two sides of the family were united."

"Did that mean the Wars of the Roses were over?" asked Sam.

"Yes, and during Henry VII's reign a completely different England was to grow into importance. As I have told you, ever since the Norman Conquest the kings and nobles of England and France had been competing for each other's lands... remember lands meant wealth. However, from now on much more wealth was being created by traders, particularly those in the wool trade. The known world was rapidly changing as new lands were discovered by sea voyages. From now on, our story of England is not going to be just about a few rich people and their ambitions, it is more a story of other clever, adventurous, and more ordinary, people. Our monarchs still had an important part to play, and parliament too, but also a new 'reformation of religious thinking' was coming about and all together it made an enormous impact on the new round world."

"The round world! Didn't they know the world was round?" asked Sam.

"No they did not, but their ignorance did not last long as you will soon find out... and that's as far as I can go today. For next time you can both choose something about The Tudors to tell me, they are the next Royal Family and we'll see where the facts that you've chosen, fit into England's Story."

"Anything, Grandpa?"

"Yes, anything you like."

CHAPTER 10

THE TUDORS

Henry VII 1485–1509
Henry VIII 1509–1547 and Edward VI 1547–1553

S.D.B

"Now England's story moves into the years of the 'Tudors'... you remember I hope that Henry Tudor, Earl of Richmond had defeated Richard III at the Battle of Bosworth in 1485?" ... it was Sam and Nikki's grandfather who was talking to the twins once again . They were all sitting once more in the peace and quiet of his country garden.

"Yes Grandpa, and he became Henry VII," said Sam.

"Quite right; I believe both of you were going to find out something about the 'Tudors' for me to fit into our story... what did you find I wonder?"

"I found out that the next king after Henry VII was Henry VIII, and he had six wives," said Nikki.

"Yes he did, but not all at the same time of course," said her grandfather. "What did you discover Sam?"

"... that all three of Henry VIII's children eventually became monarchs of England," he replied.

"Correct in every detail!" said his grandfather, "You've both done well, but let's start at the beginning; that means I must tell you about Henry VII."

"Excuse me Grandpa, but did he reign a long time like Henry VI?" asked Nikki.

"No, only half as long but he was much more successful. He was a much cleverer man and he realised that he could gain for himself, and England, more money and influence by the <u>threat</u> of war than by waging war itself."

"That was a good thing," said Sam. "I imagine that since the Wars of the Roses were over, the people wanted a bit of peace anyway."

"Yes, I'm sure you are right."

"Did anyone try to cause a rebellion against him?" asked Sam.

"There were two attempts both financed by Richard III's sister, who was the Duchess of Burgundy, but they came to nothing. One of the two rebels pretended to be the youngest of the 'Princes in the Tower', whom Richard III had killed."

"... but the people knew that they were dead, didn't they?" said Nikki.

"Yes, most probably they did. The first rebel was captured and given a job in the royal kitchens; the second was a bit more of a nuisance to Henry VII and so when he was captured he was executed in the Tower. To make his own position as secure as possible Henry let it be known to his English subjects, that no one would be dispossessed of their lands if they gave him their support. He also made good friends in other countries; he made an alliance with the King of Spain in 1489, by arranging a future marriage between his eldest son, Prince Arthur, and the Spanish princess, Catherine of Aragon. A few years later he arranged for his daughter Margaret to marry the King of Scotland and thereby bring some peace to the borderlands in the north of England."

"He seems to have been quite a sensible man," said Nikki.

"I think so too... and these last years of the fifteenth century were an important time in the history of the world... can either of you tell me the name of a famous sailor who discovered a new land in 1492?"

Christopher Columbus

The children looked a bit puzzled, so their grandfather added, "His first name was Christopher; does that help?"

"Not Christopher Columbus?" said Sam.

"Yes!"

"... and the new land must have been America," said Nikki.

"Yes again, well done!"

"There were lots of voyages of discovery about this time, as I think I've mentioned before."

"Why just at this time Grandpa?" asked Sam.

"Well, I must just go back a bit to 1453 to answer that. In that year the Muslim, Turkish armies captured the Christian city of Constantinople and so they then controlled the land trading routes to and from the eastern lands. Do you know where that city is? It's called a different name today... Istanbul. Let me show you where it is on the map and you will see why it was so important."

"Look there it is... just where Europe joins on to Asia."

"So you can see why the Christian countries of Western Europe [mainly Portugal, England, Holland and Spain] decided to try to find sea routes to what they called the 'Indies'. Christopher Columbus sailed westwards and found [not the Indies, but America]; John Cabot, with the help of some money from Henry VII, did the same and found Newfoundland in 1497.

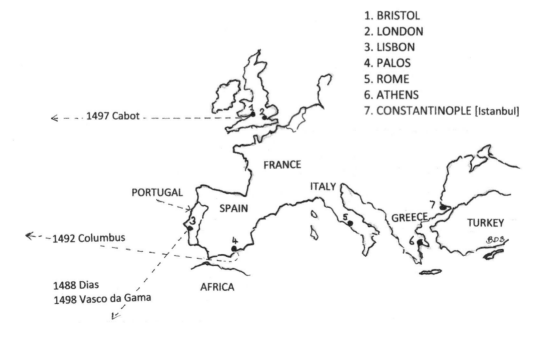

1. BRISTOL
2. LONDON
3. LISBON
4. PALOS
5. ROME
6. ATHENS
7. CONSTANTINOPLE [Istanbul]

1497 Cabot

FRANCE

PORTUGAL

SPAIN

ITALY

GREECE

TURKEY

1492 Columbus

1488 Dias
1498 Vasco da Gama

AFRICA

One year later Vasco da Gama from Portugal sailed southwards around Africa and found India, and in 1519 another Portuguese sailor, Ferdinand Magellan, began a voyage that was the first to sail right around the world... proving that the world was indeed round."

"He must have been the most famous of them all," said Sam.

"I'm sure he would have been but for the fact that he was killed during the voyage, which was completed by his crew; I'm afraid only 18 men survived out of more than 200 that started that voyage."

"This doesn't sound much like 'England's Story' to me," said Sam, "...apart from John Cabot," he added.

"You'll soon see how it all fits in," replied his grandfather, "but now let's go back to Henry VII again. "

"Did he build any new colleges like Henry VI?" asked Nikki.

"No, I don't think so, but I believe he helped to make sure the work continued on those places... he himself ordered, in 1503, the building of the beautiful chapel on the east end of Westminster Abbey that still bears his name, and which we will visit when we go to see Westminster Hall. Henry VII was buried in his chapel when he died in 1509... and of course you both know who comes next."

"Henry VIII!" they both said.

"Yes, that's right; no more 'boy kings' for a while anyway. Henry VIII was a tall handsome fellow eighteen years old, and had been well educated. Of course if his elder brother Prince Arthur had not died in 1502, he would not have been king at all... Henry would probably have been made a bishop."

"We might have had a _real_ King Arthur at last," said Nikki.

"We might indeed. I think Henry VII, being a Welshman, probably thought that by naming his first son Arthur, Prince of Wales, he would keep his support in that country."

"Grandpa, didn't you say it was Arthur, who was going to marry the Princess of Spain?" said Sam.

"Yes, Prince Arthur and Princess Catherine of Aragon did get married in 1501; sadly he died just five months later. Henry VII was anxious to keep Catherine's dowry, so a new plan was devised for his second son to marry her instead."

"Excuse me Grandpa, but what's a dowry?" asked Nikki.

"It is the gift of land, money or possessions, which are given by the parents of a bride to the husband or family of the bridegroom," he replied, "it has long gone out of fashion in England."

"Oh, I see," said Nikki.

"What happened to Catherine?" asked Sam.

"She continued to live in England whilst her father and her father-in-law argued about the dowry. As soon as Henry VII died, Henry VIII did marry Catherine, but he had to get the Pope's permission, because she had already been married to his brother."

"Were there any rebellions against Henry VIII?" asked Sam, changing the subject.

"Not really," his grandfather replied, "he had a much easier time than his father, and thanks to him, he had a lot of money and lands which he inherited... and he set out to enjoy life. Firstly, he decided to help his new father-in-law [the King of Spain] to fight a war against France; this in turn caused the Scots to invade England with disastrous results."

"Why?" asked Nikki, "do tell us what happened, Grandpa."

"The Scots, who were traditionally friends of France, thought that whilst Henry was away fighting in France and Catherine was in England on her own, it would be easy to invade our country. However the Earl of Surrey, whom Henry had left in charge, defeated them at the Battle of Flodden in 1513 and the Scottish King was killed. The Queen of Scotland

Battlefield of Flodden ...today

69

was Henry's sister Margaret, so after that, he was confident that while she was in charge, the Scots would not cause him any more trouble. One year later peace was made with France and the French agreed to pay Henry lots of money provided that he didn't invade again."

"I can see that he was quite lucky," said Nikki.

"He was lucky in another way too," continued her grandfather, "for he appointed a very clever man called Thomas Wolsey to be his Lord Chancellor — he also made him Archbishop of York — and more or less allowed him to govern the country for him, but problems arose between them in 1525."

"What sort of problems, Grandpa?" asked Sam.

"Problems connected with Queen Catherine. Henry and Catherine had had six children but only one survived; she was Princess Mary, and Henry desperately wanted a son to succeed him. By 1525 Queen Catherine was too old to have any more children, so Henry asked Wolsey to see if the Pope would allow him to divorce Catherine and marry again. Actually Henry VIII had already fallen in love with one of Catherine's ladies-in-waiting called Anne Boleyn. Anne happened to be very much in favour of the new 'reformed religious thinking' that was starting to influence many people within Europe."

Hever Castle, Kent, restored 1903. Original home of Anne Boleyn

The entrance to Hampton Court Palace

"I think the king did have his divorce, "said Nikki, "because I know he eventually had six wives."

"Yes he did, but the Pope would not permit it and Henry was very angry. He blamed his friend Cardinal Wolsey, who was also the Pope's official representative in England for his difficulties, and ordered his arrest. Wolsey died while on his way to prison in London and Henry confiscated his home called Hampton Court Palace. He also ordered that Queen Catherine and their daughter Princess Mary should be banished from all his palaces."

"What did the Pope do?" asked Sam.

"He decided to punish Henry, but Henry quickly got the English parliament to pass a law making it high treason for anyone to obey the Pope, and at the same time all the money that was usually sent to the Pope from England was stopped. Finally he appointed Thomas Cranmer to be Archbishop of Canterbury and he gave the king the divorce he wanted."

"So he married Anne Boleyn?"

"Yes, in 1533, and a short while later the future Queen Elizabeth was born."

"Was Henry pleased?" asked Nikki.

"No, not very. You must remember that up to this time there had never been a ruling Queen of England, so he still desperately wanted a son to succeed him. In the mean time however, because his eldest child, Princess Mary, was a Catholic like her mother, a law was passed which required everyone over twenty-one to swear that the baby Princess Elizabeth should be his heir. His Lord Chancellor Sir Thomas More, who had succeeded Cardinal Wolsey, was one of the people who refused to do this, and so eventually he was beheaded. A short time later Queen Anne Boleyn was accused of misbehaviour, and on Henry's orders she too was tried and executed in the same way."

"Gosh!" said Sam, "it seems that it was a very dangerous time to live!"

"It was indeed," said his grandfather. "Henry VIII immediately married another young lady called Jane Seymour, and finally they had a baby son, Prince Edward born in 1536."

"So all was now OK perhaps?" said Nikki.

"It might have been, but Queen Jane died only nine days after her son was born, so all Henry's rejoicing turned to sadness."

"But he didn't need another wife, did he?" asked Nikki.

"No, you're right, he didn't. Eventually, however his advisers thought it would be a good idea for the country if he were to marry again. On the advice of Thomas Cromwell, his new chancellor since the death of Sir Thomas More, he agreed to marry a German princess, whose name was Anne of Cleves. Unfortunately when they first met, he did not like her <u>at all</u> and very quickly another sort of divorce was arranged. Thomas Cromwell was blamed and soon suffered the same fate as Sir Thomas More."

"Do you mean he was beheaded?" asked Sam.

"Yes."

"Did Henry fight any battles?" asked Sam, who was a bit bored with all the stories about wives.

"It is interesting that you should ask me that," replied his grandfather, "because some very important so-called 'battles' were being fought throughout his reign, but not the sort I imagine you were thinking about."

"What were they, Grandpa?" [Sam was intrigued]

"They were 'battles of conscience', between the traditional and the new ways of thinking about religion. As I have already mentioned, Henry's replacement as chancellor after Sir Thomas More's execution was Thomas Cromwell, and he, and Queen Anne Boleyn and Queen Jane and Queen Anne of Cleves were all of the new thinking... and so was Henry... up to a point. Also I must tell you that between 1536 and 1540 all the nunneries and monasteries in England were 'dissolved' and their possessions and lands were kept by the king or sold by him to raise money. Henry himself ordered that Bibles printed in English should be placed in every parish church."

A chained Bible of Henry VIII

"Gosh, didn't they already have Bibles?" asked Nikki.

"Only ones written in Latin, which priests could understand," said her grandfather, "this is why the invention of 'printing', which had been brought over to England sixty-three years earlier by William Caxton, was so important."

"But could ordinary people read?" continued Nikki.

"Probably not, but there were lots of people who could read to them, I expect."

Nikki wanted to know a bit more about Henry's wives, because she had remembered there were six, so she interrupted to ask, "Grandpa, what happened to Anne of Cleves please?"

"Henry's marriage to her was 'annulled', which means 'made as if it did not happen' and she was given various large estates (including Hever Castle) where she lived out the rest of her days with a pension from the king."

"So, what happened next?"

"Some nobles of the traditional religious thinking, decided to try to influence the King by introducing him to a young Catholic lady of their family. Her name was Catherine Howard; she was just 22 years old, and she soon became wife number five. I'm afraid to say she misbehaved with another lover and within a year of their marriage the second Queen Catherine suffered the same fate as Queen Anne Boleyn."

"Oh, no!" exclaimed Nikki, "that's awful... but there was still one more wasn't there."

"Yes, she was Katherine Parr and married Henry in 1543... she outlived the King, who died in 1547. She was kind to Henry in his last years and a good stepmother to all his children. After Henry's death she herself married again for her fourth time, to a man called Thomas Seymour, he was the brother of Queen Jane Seymour... Katherine died one year after Henry in 1548. Now, children, who do you think was the new king?"

"Edward... but how old was he, Grandpa?"

"He was nine."

"I expect his uncles ruled for him, if he had uncles? Were there the usual problems again?" asked Sam.

"Yes, as you know from our story so far, there were always difficulties when a young king came to the throne," replied his grandfather, "and so it was again. It was his mother's other brother, Edward Seymour who became his 'Protector'. He was a well meaning man and was given the title of Duke of Somerset. Like the King, he was strongly in favour of the new religion. He and those of a similar thinking were given the nick-name 'Protestors'... or 'Protestants', which describes them even today."

"Was Henry VIII's archbishop still alive?" asked Nikki, "the one who gave him his first divorce?"

"Yes indeed he was. You may be interested to know that it was he, Thomas Cranmer, and Edward Seymour, Duke of Somerset, who organised the writing of the first 'Book of Common Prayer', which was introduced by law in 1549, and this caused the first of those difficulties I mentioned."

Archbishop Thomas Cramer writing the Book of Common Prayer

Edward VI aged 13, and his signature

"Was it rebellions?" asked Sam.

"Yes, rebellions began in several places. Not only that, but the Protector's own brother Thomas Seymour plotted against him."

"The one who had married Queen Katherine Parr?"

"Yes."

"What did the Duke of Somerset do?" asked Nikki.

"He had Thomas captured and executed."

"Gosh! His own brother," exclaimed Nikki.

"Yes, I agree it does seem a bit extreme," replied her grandfather, however I must tell you that Edward VI was known to be not very well, so already, powerful people were trying to guess who might succeed him... people wondered if it would be Princess Mary a traditional Catholic, or would it be Princess Elizabeth, who was a Protestant like her mother Anne Boleyn? It mattered very much, especially to the Earl of Warwick, another leader of the Protestants, who had defeated the rebellions I've just mentioned. He decided he would take over the government on behalf of King Edward VI and had the Duke of Somerset executed in his turn!"

"They were very fond of executions weren't they," said Sam, "how did it all turn out?"

"Well poor King Edward died at the age of fifteen in 1553, and for a few days only, the Earl of Warwick, who had now become the Duke of Northumberland, tried to stop Princess Mary taking the crown, by proclaiming his own daughter-in-law, Lady Jane Grey, as Queen Jane, because she was a protestant."

"So what did the people think?" asked Nikki.

"They were in favour of obeying Henry VIII's wishes regarding his children and supported Mary, who almost at once became Queen Mary. She was the first woman to rule England in her own right... and that seems to me to be a good place to stop."

"Oh, must we?" said Sam.

"If we can't go on any longer now, can we find out something for next time?" asked Nikki.

"Yes,... you can both find out about something which occurred in the next reign, that of Mary's sister Queen Elizabeth... shall I say, the Spanish Armada?" said her grandfather.

"What is an armada, Grandpa?" asked Nikki.

"It is an enormous fleet of warships."

"I shall like to do that," said Sam.

Execution axe and block

76

CHAPTER 11

THE TUDORS Part 2

Queen Mary I 1553–1558
Queen Elizabeth I 1558–1603

The two children quite enjoyed finding out about the Spanish Armada and could not wait to tell their grandfather what they had discovered... but they had to, because it was some time before they all met up together again. Nikki asked Sam what he had found out...

"I'll tell you, if you'll tell me your discovery," said Sam.

"I found out that the commander of the English fleet was..."

"I know that," said Sam, "it was Sir Francis Drake!"

"Wrong!" said Nikki.

"Who was it then?" said Sam.

"It was Lord Howard of Effingham," replied Nikki.

"Oh... I wonder if Grandpa knows that?"

"I expect so," said Nikki, "most people think it was Sir Francis Drake, because of the story that he decided to continue playing a game of bowls on Plymouth Hoe even when the first Spanish ships were sighted. What did you find out Sam?"

Sir Francis Drake's statue in Plymouth

"I found out that the fighting went on for many days and that in the end both fleets ran out of ammunition, eventually a great gale blew up and the Spanish armada escaped by sailing around Scotland and Ireland back to Spain. However, many of their galleons were wrecked on the way."

That's interesting," said Nikki, "I wonder how soon we'll get to that part of England's Story?"

Nikki did not have to wait too long, for the days went past and the time came when the twins parents had to go away for a weekend, and their grandparents were going to come and stay with them in their home.

The twins' parents leave for a weekend away

"Bye Mum, bye Dad," they called out as their parents drove away.

"Be good," their mother had reminded them, "help Granny and Grandpa as much as you can, won't you?"

"Oh, yes we will," the twins had replied.

Later that day when they were all together after tea, Nikki said, "We <u>did</u> find out some things about the Spanish Armada Grandpa."

"Oh, good. Does that mean you want to do some more of England's Story?"

"Yes please", they both said.

"I'm afraid you'll have to remind me where we got to," said their grandfather.

"You had just told us that Princess Mary Tudor had become Queen Mary," said Sam...

"... and I hoped you could tell us a bit more about Lady Jane Grey," said Nikki.

"Ah, yes. Well as far as Lady Jane Grey goes it is not a happy story I'm afraid, for it was not long after Mary became Queen, that there was a sort of Protestant rebellion which failed, as a result of which both Jane and her husband were executed in the Tower and even Princess Elizabeth was kept there for a while... soon after, things began to go from bad to worse for Mary."

"Why was that?" asked Sam.

"Remember that Mary's mother had been Spanish and like her, Mary was a convinced Catholic. Her one aim, now that she was Queen, was to restore England to the Catholic faith, so she immediately reversed all the laws of her Protestant brother Edward VI. Anyone who did not submit to the new strict Catholic ways was arrested and the punishment was to be burnt at the stake. People executed in this manner even included three bishops of the English church, one of which was the old Archbishop of Canterbury, Thomas Cranmer. They were all put to death in the town of Oxford. In total during Mary's short reign over two hundred and fifty Protestants died because they refused to change their religious thinking."

"How awful!" said Nikki.

"Was it a new punishment to be burnt to death?" asked Sam.

"No, remember that Joan of Arc had been burnt to death in France more than one hundred years before in 1431," replied his grandfather. "Burning, was nearly always the punishment for what were considered to be the most serious religious offences."

Nikki decided to change the subject, "Did Mary ever have a husband?" she asked.

"Yes she did; she married Philip, the heir to the Spanish throne, in Winchester Cathedral in 1554, but they had no children. He was the same Philip who later sent the Spanish Armada against England in 1588."

Winchester Cathedral

79

"Mary wasn't Queen for very long, was she?" asked Sam.

"No, only for five years; she died on 17th November 1558 at the age of forty-six," his grandfather replied. "Her own choice of an Archbishop of Canterbury, the Catholic Cardinal Pole, died on the same day!"

"How strange," said Nikki, "but I suppose it made it easier for the new Queen Elizabeth."

"Yes, I think it did. She chose Matthew Parker, a well-respected churchman, who had been one of her mother's chaplains. By the way, who can remember the name of the new queen's mother?"

"Anne Boleyn," both the children replied.

"You're both getting too good at answering my questions," said their grandfather. "The new queen was clever too, she could speak six languages."

"Wow!" said Sam.

"Did all the religious and church things change back again?" asked Nikki.

"Yes, more or less. The Queen chose a clever man, William Cecil, to be her chancellor and with the help of Archbishop Parker, he guided her to restore the Protestant religion in such a way as to cause as little offence to the traditional Catholics as possible."

"I don't think she ever got married," said Nikki.

"No, you are quite right, but she did fall in love a couple of times I think," said her grandfather, "and she managed to control her courtiers in England and other countries too, to some extent, by keeping everyone guessing as to whom she might marry. Mary's husband Philip was the first person to ask her to marry him, which of course she wisely refused."

"Any rebellions?" asked Sam, as usual.

"Only after 1569; this was the year when Elizabeth was asked by her cousin Mary, Queen of Scots, if she could come to live in England."

"Why did Mary have to leave Scotland?" asked Nikki.

"Well once again it was because of a conflict between the new Protestant faith and Mary's friends who were Catholics ... there was civil war in Scotland and Mary lost. Mary had to leave her one year old son James in Scotland, who then became their new king, James VI. This little boy is important in our story as you will soon find out... but of course first of all, there is much more for me to tell you about the reign of Queen Elizabeth... and for you to tell me!"

"I hope we can," said Nikki, " because that bit about Mary's son sounds interesting."

"What comes next?" asked Sam. "Was it the Armada, or did Mary go back to Scotland?"

"Neither I'm afraid," replied his grandfather, "Mary became Elizabeth's prisoner and eventually there was a plot against Elizabeth's life by Mary's Catholic friends in England and very reluctantly Elizabeth agreed to Mary's execution. The situation was very difficult for Elizabeth because all the Catholic countries of Europe were against England and she had to expect there might be a war because of her decision."

Bolton Castle, Yorkshire.
The place of detention of Mary Queen of Scots

"I think that means we must be coming soon to the Armada," said Sam.

"Yes that's right, in 1588 Philip II of Spain decided to help the Pope restore Catholicism to England by force. The plan was for the armada to sail from Spain to pick up extra troops from the Spanish Netherlands and then invade England."

"Where were the Spanish Netherlands Grandpa?" asked Nikki.

"They were what today we call Belgium and Holland."

"So, if the Armada was defeated, no extra soldiers could come to England," said Sam and then he added, "how did the English know about the Spanish plans, Grandpa?".

"From the reports of spies, I expect," said his grandfather. "Queen Elizabeth had a very good 'spymaster' by the name of Sir Francis Walsingham... it was his job to find out all he could about the enemies of the queen both in England and abroad."

"I found out the name of the English admiral in charge of our ships," said Nikki.

"Please tell me," said her grandfather.

"It was Lord Howard of Effingham."

"It was indeed. Most people think it was Sir Francis Drake, but he was only the Vice-admiral, even though he had been the first Englishman to sail right around the world in 1576 in his ship called the 'Golden Hind'."

"Do you know how many ships there were in the Spanish Armada?" asked Sam.

"I think it was about one hundred and thirty, of which seventy-two were real fighting ships and the rest were to be used just to transport the Spanish troops," replied his grandfather.

The Armada is in sight

"How many ships did we have?"

"About half as many, but our ships had longer range guns, so that meant the English fleet could fire cannon-balls at the enemy ships before they could fire back."

"That was 'cool', wasn't it?" said Sam

"Yes, it was very important. Not one English ship was lost during the fighting."

"I bet people thought it was a bit of a miracle, when they heard about it," said Nikki.

"Actually they knew about it very quickly, because some of the fighting happened in sight of people standing on the cliffs along the English Channel coast. One night, the Spanish admiral ordered his ships to anchor off the French coast, whereupon the English set fire to some of their own ships and let them drift down towards the Spanish fleet. This caused panic in the enemy ships as they tried desperately to sail out of the way."

"Then, I found out that a great storm came," said Sam, "and they could only escape by sailing northwards and around Scotland and Ireland to get back to Spain, so they never picked up the Spanish soldiers and there was no invasion."

"I'm sure Queen Elizabeth was very thankful," said Nikki.

"She certainly was, and suddenly England was regarded as a major power in the world. Her sailors had increased confidence in their ability, and from this time they began to develop the trading links that eventually created the British Empire."

"Were there any more battles at sea during Elizabeth's reign?" asked Sam.

"There certainly were," replied his grandfather. "The war was not over and English sailors attacked the Spanish ships wherever they could find them, often capturing vast treasures and becoming very rich."

Shakespeare's Globe Theatre built 1599... rebuilt 1997

"How long did Queen Elizabeth reign?" asked Nikki.

"For forty-five years, and it was towards the end of her reign that England's greatest poet began to write his plays. I'm sure you know who I'm talking about?"

"Was it William Shakespeare?" asked Sam.

"Yes, well done. England was a much more peaceful place after the Armada was defeated and those people with great wealth began to use it to build fine mansions and also playhouses; sometimes they used it to finance new adventures to faraway places like India. They started new companies... the East India Company for example in 1600; this company will come into our story again as the years go by."

"Was Sir Francis Drake one of them?" asked Sam.

"No, sadly he died at sea in 1596, still seeking ways of attacking the Spanish colonies in the West Indies."

"If Queen Elizabeth never married," said Nikki, "how did they decide who was going to succeed her?"

"Although the queen did not like to talk about it, it is likely that the advice of Robert Cecil, who was her chief minister at the end of her reign, encouraged her to consider the claim of James, the Protestant son of Mary Queen of Scots, who was already King James VI of Scotland. When Elizabeth died in 1603 he <u>did</u> become James I of England as well. For the first time ever there was one king to reign over both countries."

"Did the English mind having a Scottish king?" asked Sam.

"I don't think so; most peoples' concern was to have a king who was not a Catholic, replied his grandfather."

"But they didn't know much about him, did they?" asked Sam. "He could have been dreadful."

"Some people probably thought he was, but to start with, James was very careful to try not to offend his new subjects. He had known from Robert Cecil about his chances of becoming king of the rich country of England for a few years. I always wonder if Queen Elizabeth privately agreed to him succeeding her as a way of making amends for ordering the execution of his mother... we'll never know."

"It is a nice thought," said Nikki.

"I think that's where we will stop for today," added her grandfather, "we can begin the new 17th century and the new King James I, sometime tomorrow."

"Is there anything we can try to find out about him?" asked Sam.

"Let me think... Yes, there is a connection between James I and the Bible; I wonder if you can find out what it is?"

"We'll have a good try, Grandpa," said Nikki.

GOLDEN HIND
A replica of the ship in which Sir Francis Drake sailed around the world

CHAPTER 12

THE STUARTS

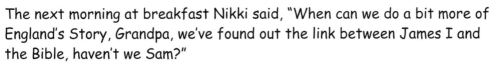

James I 1603–1625
Charles I and the Civil War 1625–1649

The next morning at breakfast Nikki said, "When can we do a bit more of England's Story, Grandpa, we've found out the link between James I and the Bible, haven't we Sam?"

"Well, we're pretty certain," said Sam.

"I think sometime after tea would be best, because your grandmother and I are thinking of taking you to Salisbury today."

"That will be great!" said Nikki. "I can wait until then easily."

So the day out was planned and they all had a good time. They had lunch in a restaurant in the forecourt of a military museum in the Cathedral Close. It had been named after a place in France, which had been the first village to be liberated on the 'D Day Invasion' during the Second World War. From its windows they could see the enormous spire of the cathedral pointing up into the blue sky.

"Are we going into the cathedral to see the copy of Magna Carta?" asked Sam.

"We are," was the reply; and they did.

As they came out again into the sunshine, Nikki said," It's nice to be inside such an old building and to feel part of the real history of that time."

"I liked the effigy of the knight in armour lying on his tomb," said Sam.

Tomb and effigy of Sir William Longespee in Salisbury Cathedral

Back at home again, tea was finished, and the two children settled down to listen to some more of England's Story as told by their grandfather. "First of all," he said, "can you remember the year that James I succeeded Queen Elizabeth?"

"1603," they both said together.

"Excellent, so here we are at the beginning of one of the most interesting centuries in our story... which century was it?"

"The 17th Century," said Sam.

"I knew that too," said Nikki.

"Of course you did; it was a bit of an easy question I know," said their grandfather. "Now where shall I begin?" he said thoughtfully, "... how about a bit of a bang!"

"A bang?" said Sam.

"Well, nearly a bang... can you guess what I'm thinking about?"

Both the children shook their heads.

"Guy Fawkes and the Gunpowder Plot."

"Gosh, was that at this time?" said Nikki.

"It was indeed. Have you heard the rhyme,'

Guy Fawkes caught beneath the House of Lords

Please do remember
The 5th of November,
Gunpowder, treason and plot.
We know of no reason,
Why gunpowder treason
should ever be forgot.

It was poor King James and his entire parliament that Guy Fawkes and his colleagues tried to kill."

"They were discovered just in time to prevent any explosion, weren't they?" said Sam.

"Yes, the Gunpowder Plot happened in 1605, only eighteen months after James became king. As I think I mentioned before, Queen Elizabeth had managed to keep the religious extremists of both Catholic and Protestant faiths under control during her reign, but there were still many people who couldn't accept the views of their religious opponents, and this is where both the Gunpowder Plot and the information you have found out are part of the story. Almost the first thing the Protestant religious leaders asked King James, was if there could be...", their grandfather paused...

"... a new Bible," said Nikki quickly.

"It was authorised, by King James in 1604," added Sam.

"... and completed in 1609," continued Nikki.

"... and ever since it has been known as 'The Authorised Version' or 'The King James Bible'," said Sam.

"You certainly did your homework," said their grandfather. "Do you know it was printed in 1611 and is still in use today? I expect King James hoped it would provide a basis for agreement among the religious groups," he added.

"Did it?"

"I believe it did; gradually it found a use in all countries of the world where English people settled."

"What happened to the Gunpowder Plot conspirators?" asked Sam.

"Since the penalty for treason was death, they were sentenced to be 'hung, drawn and quartered'... it was an awful way to die."

"What does 'quartered' mean Grandpa," asked Sam.

" After death their bodies were chopped up into four pieces."

"It seems to me that the terrible executions of Mary's reign were beginning all over again," said Nikki.

"Yes, it does seem like that, but you must realise that there were similar executions in Elizabeth's reign just the same, especially during the war with Spain, when all Catholics were under suspicion for being spies for the enemy."

Map of JAMESTOWN in Virginia USA

"Grandpa," said Sam, "was it in James I's reign that there was the 'Mayflower' adventure to America?"

"Yes, indeed, you're quite right. The king encouraged people to form more companies like the East India Company and a new one in 1606 was called the 'Virginia Company'. In 1607 they made the first English settlement in America at 'Jamestown'... called after the king of course!"

"Why was it called the 'Mayflower'," asked Nikki.

"Mayflower was the name of the biggest of the three ships that sailed with 'The Pilgrim Fathers' [as they became known] in the year 1620. The settlers were very strict Protestants, called Puritans, who wanted to leave England because the Church of England [though a Protestant church] was not "pure" enough for them."

The MAYFLOWER arrives in America 1620

"James I didn't mind them going then," said Nikki.

"No, as I've just said, he encouraged them, because once established in the new lands they would need supplies and things from England, and all the trading taxes from the ports were given to the king," replied her grandfather.

"Were there any other settlements started during James reign?" asked Nikki.

"Yes, one was begun in Bermuda in 1609 and another one in 1623 on the island of St. Christophe in the West Indies, from where sugar was a very valuable export."

"I think I heard that tobacco and potatoes came from Virginia," said Sam, "and that there were other newly discovered things too."

"Yes, you are correct," replied his grandfather, "tobacco smoking was thought to be healthy! Of course we know better today," he added.

"Did King James I have any children?" asked Nikki.

"He did, about eight or nine I think, but only three lived to be grown up. Henry the eldest died before his father, Elizabeth married the King of Bohemia, and that left Charles, who succeeded him in 1625 as Charles I."

"Where was Bohemia Grandpa?" asked Nikki.

"Today we call it the Czech Republic... it's a country in the middle of Europe."

"Was Charles I another young king with uncles?" asked Sam.

"No, he was twenty-five and was already married to a French princess called Henrietta Maria."

"So that was good, I suppose," said Nikki.

"It certainly should have been," said her grandfather, "but unfortunately things don't always work out as we might hope. James I had made peace with Spain, but his son Charles I wanted war with them!"

"Not again!" said Sam.

"I'm afraid so... this time it was the English, who sent a fleet and an army to Spain, but like the Spanish Armada, the English expedition ended in failure, and the King's best friend the Duke of Buckingham, who was in charge, was impeached by parliament."

"I'm sorry to ask, but please what does impeached mean?" asked Nikki.

"Impeached, means being held responsible by parliament for wasting the country's money, or impairing the country's reputation. The Duke of Buckingham's impeachment created the bad feeling between parliament and the King that with other arguments, eventually led to the Civil War."

"Gosh, so it was important then," said Sam.

"It was," agreed his grandfather, "and parliament went further by restricting the king's income from the proceeds of the customs dues to only one year, rather than for his whole life... at the same time they encouraged him to make war against the King of France, who was his father-in-law."

"How did he get money to run the country?" asked Sam.

"He used all sorts of different ways to raise taxes, which generally were resented by the people, and in the end he decided to govern without parliament... but of course with very little money he had to make peace with both France and Spain."

"That was a good result," said Nikki.

"Yes it was, and England was at peace for about eleven years between 1628 and 1639."

"Did Charles I do everything himself?" asked Sam.

"No, that would have been impossible; fortunately he had the help of two very able men, one was a former M.P., named Thomas Wentworth, whom he made Earl of Strafford, and the other was William Laud, his Archbishop of Canterbury. Sadly, both men, though well-intentioned, failed to appreciate the situation of the king and things went gradually from bad to worse."

"How did it come to be a civil war between the King and the Parliament?" asked Nikki.

"There were lots of causes...for a start, in 1636 Archbishop Laud persuaded Charles I that since both Scotland and England now had the same king, they should both use the same prayer book. The Scots however, had their own more strict Protestant religion, [they were known as Presbyterians] and in 1638 they created a rebellion when they were told they must use the English prayer book. The Scots formed an army and in 1640 they invaded the north of England. Charles gathered what few

89

Old Bridge, Berwick on Tweed

troops he could and faced them at Berwick and by offering a payment to the Scots he managed to prevent them coming any further... the only problem was, he didn't <u>have</u> the money he had promised to give them, so he had to call the Parliament to get some."

"Did they allow him any money?" asked Sam.

"Not straight away; first they wanted their revenge on the king's adviser the Earl of Strafford, who had helped the king to rule without parliament for so long... they impeached him and demanded his execution before they would grant the king more money; the king had no choice but to sign his friend's death warrant."

"Couldn't the king have refused?" said Nikki.

"Yes I suppose he could, but he realised civil war was now a possibility and thought he would try and prevent it by giving in. The next year, 1642, the king tried to arrest some of the members of parliament who were particularly hostile to him and led a group of soldiers to the House of Commons."

"What happened then?" asked Sam.

"The men he wanted to arrest were warned the king was coming and escaped down the River Thames to the City of London," replied his grandfather.

The escape of MPs from Charles I

"I thought that the Parliament was in London," said Nikki.

"Of course it is today, but in those days Westminster, where the Parliament sat, was separated from London by fields and there were only a few houses in between."

"Did the King chase them to London?" asked Sam.

"No, London was already on the side of Parliament and it was now Charles' turn to escape! He and his family fled first to Hampton Court, and then eventually to York. From this moment on, Charles I realised that if he wanted to regain power, he would have to fight for it."

"Did he now have enough money for an army?" asked Sam.

"Not really; in order to get some, he had to send his Queen to Europe to sell the crown jewels; other wealthy nobles who joined him paid for their own troops. The war started in 1643 and there were battles all over the country, some big, some small, but after the Battle of Naseby in 1646 the Royalists, or Cavaliers, as the King's troops were called, accepted their defeat by the forces of Parliament... who were called 'Roundheads', by the way."

Battlefield of Naseby ...today

"Did the Roundheads capture the King?" asked Nikki.

"Not exactly, for Charles first of all surrendered himself to the Scottish part of the Parliamentarian army at Newark, and it was not until 1647 when Parliament actually paid the Scottish troops for their help against the Royalists, that they handed him over to the representatives of the Parliament."

"Then what happened Grandpa?" asked Sam.

"Well, now that the war was over, Parliament ordered their own forces to go back to their homes, but even Parliament was short of money and they were reluctant to pay the soldiers, so the army did not disband, and their leaders, one of whom was Oliver Cromwell, decided to take the King away from the control of Parliament and into their own charge."

"Did that mean that there was a conflict between the Parliament and their own army?" asked Sam.

"Exactly... as time went by it is thought that the King and the army generals were close to working out a satisfactory agreement for peace, but it turned out that the ordinary soldiers would not accept these ideas, and the King was persuaded by the generals to "escape" to the Isle of Wight for his own safety."

"Where did he live, Grandpa?" asked Nikki.

"In Carisbrooke Castle, near the main town of Newport."

Carisbrooke Castle, Isle of Wight, place of detention of King Charles I

"Was he a prisoner there?"

"Yes, I suppose he was, but he could meet people and talk to them and he had some of his children with him. He realised as time passed that the English people were becoming dismayed by the way the army was behaving, and he rather stupidly encouraged the Scottish army to invade England again, on <u>his</u> side this time, in the hope he might be released."

"Did they invade?" asked Nikki.

"Yes they did, but General Cromwell and the English army soundly defeated them. After this Oliver Cromwell realised that if he was to survive himself, the King would have to die... his soldiers would not accept his orders otherwise. At the end of the year 1648, he sent soldiers to collect the King from the Isle of Wight and bring him to London, where a sort of trial was held and a sentence of death was passed upon him."

"Was the King taken to The Tower for his execution?" asked Sam.

The Execution of King Charles I outside the Banqueting House, London

"No," said his grandfather, "a special scaffold platform was erected in Whitehall and King Charles I was beheaded there on 30th January 1649. England was henceforth governed by Cromwell and his army."

"So there was no king anymore?" said Nikki.

"Not in England, but Charles' eldest son, who had gone to Europe with his mother, at once became King Charles II in the eyes of many people... the Scots for example immediately acclaimed him as <u>their</u> King."

"Can we look up anything about Charles II?" asked Sam.

"You can, but not just yet; I must tell you about the rule of Oliver Cromwell first, and we'll do that next time," his grandfather replied.

When the children's parents returned from their weekend away, Nikki, Sam and their grandparents were on the doorstep to meet them.

"Did you have a lovely time mum?" asked Nikki. "We've been learning all about the English civil war..."

"... and how King Charles came to be beheaded in London," interrupted Sam.

"Yes, our time away was all lovely, and I hope there will soon be a moment when you can tell your father and I all you have been told, but just at present all I need is a cup of tea," their mother replied... "I hope they've been good?" she added, turning to her mother.

"Oh yes," she answered, " we had a great time together; especially our day out in Salisbury."

"Well that's something else to hear about," said the children's father, " but I agree with your mother, let's get the cases inside and all have tea together."

Salisbury Cathedral

CHAPTER 13

THE REPUBLIC AND AFTERWARDS

Parliament and The Cromwells 1649–1660
Charles II 1660–1685   James II 1685–1688
William and Mary 1689–1694   William III 1694–1702

It was more than a week before Nikki and Sam met their grandfather again and they were able to persuade him to continue with 'England's Story'.

"You said you would tell us about Oliver Cromwell this time," said Sam, once they had all settled down in some comfy chairs.

"I can't wait," said Nikki.

"Very well, I'll try," he said. "One of the first things Oliver Cromwell had to do was to fight his former allies the Scots."

"Why was that?" asked Sam.

"Because the Scots had recognised Charles II as their new king and persuaded him to come to Scotland from The Netherlands to start the war all over again. Charles II and the Scottish army invaded England and there was a big battle at Worcester in September 1651, at which Charles' army was soundly defeated."

"What happened to Charles II?" asked Nikki.

"He escaped from the battle and after many adventures hiding from all the soldiers who were looking for him, he managed to get back to The Netherlands," replied her grandfather.

"It sounds as if he was pretty lucky," said Sam.

"He was, and you might imagine that now Charles II was gone, Oliver Cromwell could have a more relaxed time... but you would be wrong!"

"Why what happened, Grandpa?" asked Nikki.

"Cromwell and his army, called the 'New Model Army' by the way, had serious disagreements with the Parliament, and in fact in 1653 it could be said 'history repeated itself' when Oliver Cromwell took some soldiers down to the House of Commons and..."

"... just like Charles I had done?" asked Sam.

Statue of OLIVER CROMWELL outside the Houses of Parliament

"Yes exactly. He turned out all the M.P.'s and locked the door."

"So now there was no king and no parliament," said Nikki, "just Cromwell and the army."

"Yes I'm afraid so; it was not a happy time for the country. Cromwell did try to have new parliaments but they all tried to do things which Cromwell thought were not in the best interests of England. They hardly had time to meet in London than he decided to get rid of them again... he became what we call a dictator, which means he decided everything. In fact he became the very sort of ruler that he had fought to prevent Charles I becoming."

"How long did he rule England ?" asked Nikki.

"For just about seven years, because although England was in reality a republic from the time of Charles I's death in 1649, there was a couple of years when Parliament was sort of 'in charge' and then there was another couple of years after Oliver died in 1658, when his eldest son Richard became what was called 'Lord Protector' like his father, but it was soon clear that he was not able to lead the country and that the army was really the government. Eventually, most of the people were fed up with having military rule and wanted the King Charles II to return and to have a fresh Parliament."

"So what actually happened?" asked Sam.

"An officer called General Monk, who was in charge of the English army forces in Scotland, was invited to come to London by some M.P.'s to help restore order between the other parts of the army who had begun to fight each other. General Monk and his troops marched into England on 1st January 1660. When he got to London, he ordered a fresh Parliament to be elected and talks to begin with King Charles II in The Netherlands, to see if arrangements could be made for the King's return. Finally it was agreed that if the King would issue a free pardon to all those who had fought against him and his father, then only those who had signed his father's death warrant would be punished."

"So the king was restored to his throne," said Sam.

"Not only that," replied his grandfather, "but the authority of Parliament was restored over the army, which was disbanded at last. From that time to this, the chief power to govern the country has been in the hands of Parliament, with the King or Queen having only limited powers."

"You did say we could look up something about Charles II," said Nikki.

"Yes I remember," said her grandfather, "I would like you Sam, to find out what happened in London in 1665, and Nikki to find out what happened the next year. You may need a bit of time to do this, so when shall we meet again?"

"Perhaps next week at the same time," suggested Nikki.

"Yes, that will be fine."

Then she added, "I already know the answer to my question... it was the Great Fire."

"So do I," said Sam, "it was the Great Plague."

"Oh, that's very good," exclaimed their grandfather, "then try this one... who wrote a famous diary at that time and what was his normal employment?"

The GREAT FIRE OF LONDON in 1666

"You agreed, 'same time next week', Grandpa," said Nikki, when they all met again seven days later "Here we are!".

"Yes I know I did, Nikki, but I am just going to finish mowing the lawn; I don't think another few minutes will make any difference, do you?"

"No, of course not," she answered. "Shall Sam and I get some deckchairs from out of the shed and find a good place to sit?"

"Yes please."

"A little while later all three of them were again seated comfortably and ready

"I'm just going to finish mowing the lawn"

98

to continue with 'England's Story'. "Can I have an answer to my question first?" asked their grandfather, "what did you find out about the man who wrote the famous diary? First of all, his name was...?

"Samuel Pepys," said both the twins together.

"... and what about his employment?"

"He was Secretary to the Admiralty," said Sam, "but I'm not quite sure what that means," he added.

"It means," replied his grandfather, "that he had to carry out the orders of the Admirals and to supervise things to do with the navy on their behalf. It was a very important post because, although the New Model Army had been disbanded, the King and the Parliament decided that expenditure on new ships for the Royal Navy was a vital necessity to protect the country. The king's brother James, Duke of York was appointed 'Lord High Admiral'.

"Can anyone read Samuel Pepys' diary?" asked Nikki.

"Not the actual diary, because it is too precious, but there are lots of books available in libraries about his diary and most include actual copies of his writings... now I think we had better concentrate on King Charles II again."

"How long did he reign, Grandpa?" asked Sam.

"For twenty-five years, from 1660 until 1685."

"Did he have a difficult time..., I mean were there any rebellions?" Sam continued.

"No rebellions, I'm pleased to say," said his grandfather, "Don't forget almost everyone wanted him to be king."

"So it was quite easy then?" said Nikki.

"He certainly tried to make things as easy as possible; he was a merciful and tolerant man, and he worked hard to prevent his Royalist supporters in Parliament from being too harsh on his former opponents. In the end, mostly thanks to him, only eleven people were executed for their part in his father's death."

"Did he marry and have children?" asked Sam.

"Yes, is the answer to the first part of your question, and no, is partly the answer to the second, for Charles II and Queen Catherine had no children of their own, but there were one or more children born to other ladies that the king knew."

"...but they couldn't succeed to the throne, could they?" asked Sam.

"No, they could not, but there was one boy whom Charles liked very much and he gave him the title of the 'Duke of Monmouth', and he will come into our story again. Another important person of this time was the man whom Charles chose to plan the rebuilding of London after the Great Fire of 1666, which you've told me you already know about."

"Do you know his name?"

"No, Grandpa," both the children replied.

"It was Sir Christopher Wren."

"I think I've heard that he built St. Paul's Cathedral," said Nikki, "did he build the whole of London?"

St Mary-le-Bow church designed by
CHRISTOPHER WREN

"Not actually build it, but with his friend Robert Hooke, he designed and supervised much of the work on behalf of the king, including the rebuilding of over fifty churches which had been destroyed in the fire... most of them are still standing today. Both Wren and Hooke were members of a special club, which had been formed during the civil war to discuss new scientific discoveries. This club was now reformed by Charles II, who himself became a member, and it was called The Royal Society. Most of the cleverest people in England were invited to join, among them Samuel Pepys and Isaac Newton. From this time onwards, our story of England becomes as much the story of English explorers, scientists and politicians, as it does the story of kings and queens."

"If Charles II and Catherine had no children, then I suppose Charles' brother James was next in line to be king," said Sam.

"Yes, but there was a problem," replied his grandfather.

"I don't believe it!" said Nikki, with a little smile.

"Once again I'm afraid it was a matter of religious thinking; you see, although Charles was firmly a Church of England king, James was a Catholic like his mother and made no secret of it. Because of this, some M.P's even tried to persuade Charles II to nominate the Protestant Duke of Monmouth as the person who should succeed him."

"Did he?" asked Sam.

House of Sir Thomas Gresham in London – first meeting place of The Royal Society

"No he didn't; no matter what the consequences, King Charles was determined that his brother James should succeed him, and he almost provoked another armed conflict between himself and Parliament because of this attitude."

"When did you say that Charles II died, Grandpa?" asked Nikki.

"In 1685."

"So that's when James became king?"

"Yes, as James II, and everyone hoped he would be sensible about his religious views... but he wasn't, and unwisely he began to give Catholics positions of great power. Another unwise man was the Duke of Monmouth; being a Protestant he thought that the people of England would prefer him as a king, so he immediately invaded England, landed at Lyme Regis and formed an army to fight his uncle."

The arrival of the Duke of Monmouth at Lyme Regis

Battlefield Memorial at Sedgemoor

"Does that mean there was another civil war?" said Sam.

"Not really, I think we ought to call it a rebellion. There was just one battle at Sedgemoor in Somerset, which James' army won; the Duke was captured and speedily executed... this was the last land battle to be fought between Englishmen on English soil."

"Grandpa, before I forget; what happened to Richard Cromwell?" asked Sam.

"He chose to leave England for most of Charles II's reign, but he did come back in 1680 and lived modestly under a different name until well into Queen Anne's reign... now where were we?"

"Did James II have any children?" asked Nikki.

"Yes, he had two daughters by his first wife, who had died in 1671, both were strongly Protestant; Mary, who married William of Orange [the ruler of Holland] and Anne who married a Prince of Denmark. If James and his second wife had no sons, then Mary would be in line to succeed her father as Queen one day, and people felt they could perhaps put up with a Catholic king, knowing that Mary would be the next monarch. Suddenly, and some people thought suspiciously, soon after James became king, his second wife also a Catholic, bore him a son. James was very pleased but the English people were <u>not</u>, and many important people wrote secretly to Mary's husband, William of Orange to ask him to come to England with

102

Mary to help them get rid of their Catholic king James II."

"Gosh, did he come?" asked Sam.

"Yes he did. In 1688, William and his troops landed at Torbay in Devon and although James II and his army came to challenge him, many of James' officers and soldiers deserted him and offered their services to William; even the Royal Navy abandoned the king. There was no battle this time, because James soon realised that most of the people in England were against him and so he fled to France, which was a Catholic country and where his wife and new-born son had already gone."

"Does that mean William became king?" asked Nikki.

"Well he did and he didn't," said her grandfather who, seeing her puzzled expression, explained, "his wife Mary was really the rightful successor to her father, but she agreed with her husband that they should be joint monarchs, so their reign is usually called the reign of 'William and Mary'. Parliament decided that the new arrangements should be written down and that the English ideas of liberty and democracy should be made into proper laws, so they passed a 'Bill of Rights' in 1689."

"Was it like a new Magna Carta?" asked Sam.

"That's a good way of thinking about it," agreed his grandfather. "It also provided that in the event that William and Mary had no children, that Mary's sister Anne would be the next monarch. Mary actually chose to take second place to her husband whenever he was in England... which wasn't often."

"Why not Grandpa?" asked Nikki.

"Well, King James II, with the help of the King of France very quickly arrived back in Ireland, which was a Catholic country and set up a sort of government in Dublin. Since most of the population were also Catholics they welcomed him... all except in the northern counties, where a lot of Protestants had been encouraged to settle from Scotland since the time of James I. In 1690 William went to Ireland with an army and defeated King James II at the 'Battle of the Boyne', and James fled back to France. Almost at once William had to take his army to Holland to defend his own country from invading French armies, and so Mary was left in charge in England."

"How long did William and Mary rule England?" asked Nikki.

"Well, Mary II actually died in 1694, and then William III continued on his own until his death in 1702, so that makes it about fourteen years altogether," replied her grandfather.

"Apart from William's wars against France, was it peaceful in England?" asked Sam.

"Yes it was. Of course there were differences of opinion in Parliament about whether English troops should be used to fight wars in Europe, and William's reliance on his Dutch advisers didn't go down too well, but in general things were quiet. However, there was one Englishman called John Churchill, whom William trusted — he had helped him when he first came over from Holland — and he made him Earl of Marlborough. He and his wife Sarah were also very friendly with Princess Anne, who was expected to be the next Queen."

"Did James II ever try to come back again?" asked Nikki.

"No, he died in France in 1701, but matters didn't end there because the King of France announced that he considered James' son to be the rightful king of England as James III. At once all the English M.P's agreed this was unacceptable, and thought they should prepare for a possible French invasion."

"More wars then?" said Sam.

"In a way; but more about that later, now would be a good time to stop for a cup of tea I think, let's go inside and see what Granny has got for us in the kitchen."

<hr />

Nikki called out as soon as she entered the house, "Granny, we've been hearing all about King James II and King William III."

"Have you really... would you like a drink of orange and one of my special biscuits then?" said her grandmother.

"Oh! Yes please"... then she thought to herself, smiled and said, "Do you think it could be a 'Prince of Orange' drink?"

"I'll do my best; if I add some ice and a little tonic water, I think it will be a drink fit for a prince... and a princess," she quickly added.

A 'Prince of Orange' drink

CHAPTER 14

THE EIGHTEENTH CENTURY

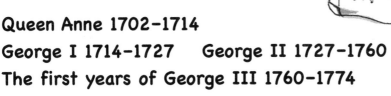

Queen Anne 1702–1714
George I 1714–1727   George II 1727–1760
The first years of George III 1760–1774

"That's better," said the twins' grandfather when they had settled down again after their drinks, "now where was I?"

"I had just asked if there was going to be another war," said Sam, "because the French   agreed that the son of James II was the rightful new King of England; so were there any wars about that?"

"Not straightaway, but everyone in the government thought it might be a better idea to try to defeat the French in Europe, rather than to wait for them to invade our country, and as soon as Anne became Queen she made her best friend's husband, John Churchill, who was already a famous soldier, the head of the British Army. His first task was to take an English army to help the Dutch and the other enemies of France, defeat the French armies in Europe, which he did with great success, winning four major battles between 1704 and 1709. To show her thanks after his first victory at Blenheim in southern Germany, Queen Anne made him Duke of Marlborough and arranged for a wonderful house to be built for him, called Blenheim Palace."

Blenheim Palace, home of the Duke of Marlborough

"I've got a friend at school who has been there," said Sam. "Can we all go there with Grandma one day?"

"I'm sure we can, it's not too far."

"My friend said that another famous member of the Churchill family in the twentieth century, Sir Winston Churchill, was born there."

"He was indeed; and after his funeral in St Paul's Cathedral in 1965, he was buried near there in the village churchyard at Bladon... which reminds me, did you know that St. Paul's Cathedral was completed during Queen Anne's reign in 1710 and there is a statue of her outside the entrance?"

Statue of Queen Anne, in front of St Paul's Cathedral

"I think so," said Nikki, "but what about Sir Christopher Wren, did he have a memorial?"

"His son had words in Latin put on his tomb, which said, ' *If you seek his memorial, look around you'*... in other words the entire building is his memorial."

" I would like to know if there was peace again after all the Duke of Marlborough's battles," said Sam.

"Yes there was a treaty in 1713, the year before Queen Anne died, and as a result England was given new lands in Canada," replied his grandfather.

"Did Queen Anne have any children, Grandpa?" asked Nikki.

"Lots, but only one little boy lived any length of time and he died in 1700, before his mother came to the throne. Parliament at once decided that a Protestant descendant of James I should be the next king after Queen Anne...the best person they could find was George, the Elector of Hanover in Germany."

"Does that mean people voted for him?" asked Sam.

"No... actually his title of 'elector' came about through a traditional historical procedure whereby certain European princes voted for the Emperor of Austria."

"Did everyone in England agree that George should succeed Anne?" asked Nikki.

"No not everyone. I think I told you James II had died in France in 1701, but there were still a few people who thought his son, whom some called James III, should be allowed to return. However, by 1714 when Queen Anne died they were not very powerful and George I was generally welcomed."

"Grandpa..."

"Yes, Sam..."

"It's funny that England has had kings from so many different countries."

"How many can you think of?"

"France ... Wales, and Scotland," said Nikki, quickly.

"Um... Holland... and Germany," added Sam.

"Don't forget Denmark ," said their grandfather. "All of them eventually became as English as the rest of us, especially the Anglo-Saxons, who of course came from Germany like King George."

"So are we a bit of all those countries as well?" asked Nikki.

"I expect so. Most of us have some ancestors from other countries in our family histories... one of my own great-grandfathers came from Ireland and another from Scotland, so actually a little bit of you is both Irish and Scottish. Now... I think we ought to go back to George I."

"Were there any rebellions against him," asked Nikki.

"Yes, there was one against him in 1715 and another against his son George II in 1745. Both began in Scotland on behalf of the exiled Stuart royal family [sometimes called The Pretenders]. By the time 'The Old Pretender' arrived in Scotland in 1715, his rebel forces had been beaten and so he sailed straight back to France again."

"Do you think the English people minded having a German king?" asked Sam.

"I think they minded a bit, because he could not speak our language, and as time went on, it seemed that he was more interested in his Hanover lands."

"If he could not speak English, how did he govern the country?" asked Nikki.

"He relied mostly upon an M.P. called Sir Robert Walpole, as did his son who became George II in 1727. Sir Robert Walpole in fact became the first real 'Prime Minister' of England, and he was the first to live in No.10, Downing Street, which I'm sure you know, is where the Prime Minister still lives today.

No 10 downing Street ...today

Walpole was a clever politician and his main aim was to keep England out of any wars that happened in Europe."

"Was he successful?" asked Sam.

"He was until 1739, when there was a strong desire in Parliament to declare war against Spain."

"Why against Spain, Grandpa?" asked Nikki.

"Spain was still a rich country and it had a weak government, which a lot of members of parliament thought they could usefully exploit. There were often quarrels between the two countries especially in the islands of the West Indies where sugar was grown."

"What does 'exploit' mean, Grandpa?" asked Sam.

"To make use of, for your own benefit', is what I should say," he replied.

"So did they gain any extra territory for our country?" asked Sam.

"Not really, Sir Robert Walpole was forced to resign in 1742 and while the new ministers of the government were sending troops against the Spanish, there was another attempt at a rebellion in 1745 to restore the Stuart family to the throne."

"What happened?"

"The Jacobites, as they were called, encouraged The Old Pretender's son, known as 'Bonnie Prince Charlie' to land in Scotland and form an army to invade England."

"Trying to start a civil war again," said Sam.

"Exactly; but although the Scots and a few English supporters did invade and eventually reached the town of Derby, there was no real

Bonnie Prince Charlie memorial… Glenfinnan, on the banks of Loch Shiel

support for them and Prince Charles Stuart ordered a retreat back to Scotland. He knew that the English soldiers were being brought back from Europe to fight him and indeed they followed him northwards. Eventually, the two sides fought the Battle of Culloden near the town of Inverness in April 1746 and Prince Charles' forces were defeated by those commanded by King George II's son, the Duke of Cumberland."

"What happened to Prince Charles?" asked Nikki.

"He managed to escape back to France and never returned again. The Scottish Highlanders, who formed most of his troops were harshly punished and English soldiers were positioned in newly-built fortresses to make sure there was no more trouble from that country again."

"What about the war against Spain? Did it go on very long?"

"About seven years."

"... and you said nobody won?" said Sam.

"Yes I <u>did</u> say that; there was a sort of peace and all the captured possessions were returned to their original owners, but the peace didn't last long. In 1755 another war broke out between England and France because of disputes in the two countries' colonial territories in America

The British Army attacking Quebec

and India. A new politician called William Pitt, was put in charge of the government, even though George II did not like him very much."

"Who was William Pitt?" asked Sam.

"He was a well-respected M.P., whose grandfather had become very rich trading in India. Although he had opposed the King's previous choice of chief ministers, it was felt by his colleagues that he was now the best man to lead the country in time of war. Battles were fought against the French in Canada where General Wolfe captured the city of Quebec, and in America, Europe, India, and on most of the

General Wolfe mortally wounded at Quebec

world's oceans, all of which brought English forces great success and great possessions... by the time of George II's death in 1760, England had become a world power."

"It seems that wars just went on and on," said Nikki.

"You're right, and it's very easy for me to focus on them and to forget to tell you about other things that happened in George II's reign, which you may have heard about."

"Like what, Grandpa?" said Sam.

The crowds listening to…

"Well for example, in 1732 the last of the American colonies was founded and it was called 'Georgia' after King George; then there was

… John Wesley

the beginning of the religious ministry of John Wesley called Methodism in 1738. I'm sure you've heard the song 'Rule Britannia'... well, that was first set to music in 1740. In 1742 came the first performance of 'The Messiah' a very famous work for chorus and orchestra composed by George Handel, which is still very popular today, and two years later our National Anthem was first published. Our calendar was altered in 1752; the British Museum was founded one year after this and then Kew Gardens were established soon after that... I think that's enough for the moment, don't you?."

"We've been to Kew Gardens," said Sam, "and I know there is a British Museum in London, but why did they have a new calendar?"

"It was to bring English dates into line with most other European countries, and it was needed because the earth travels around the sun in just a bit more than 365 days, and therefore if nothing was done the seasons of the year would gradually occur in the wrong months."

"Oh," said Nikki, "I didn't know that. Who came after George II?"

"It was his grandson who became George III, because his son Frederick had died in 1751. The new king almost immediately dismissed William Pitt in spite of his successful leadership of the country, [though he did make him Earl of Chatham] and asked a friend of his own mother, the Earl of Bute, to become his chief minister."

"Was the war over by then?" asked Nikki.

"Almost... a peace was signed with France in Paris in 1763, which allowed England to keep most of the places it had won during the war, including the whole of Canada and all of America to the east of the River Mississippi.

However once the peace with France was established, old disagreements between England and its American colonies now began to cause more and more trouble, and in 1773 the citizens of Boston in Massachusetts were so outraged by a new tax imposed by the British government on the importation of tea, that they dressed up as Indians and attacked a ship carrying tea and threw all the tea into the harbour. These actions and others led to another conflict that changed the course of world history."

Tea chests being dumped into Boston Harbour

"Gosh, what was that?" asked Sam.

"The War of American Independence,.... and if we stop our story here for the moment perhaps you can find out for next time, how long it lasted and who was the American general who became the first President of the United States," replied his grandfather.

"I think I already know the answer to the second part, but I'm not exactly sure," said Nikki... "...can we meet again soon?"

"The sooner the better," said Sam.

"I hope so too," replied their grandfather.

CHAPTER 15

THE 18th CENTURY Part 2

The final years of George III 1774–1810 including the Birth of the USA
... and the beginnings of The Industrial Revolution

Another week went by...

"Hurry up Sam, we're waiting," called Nikki to her brother.

"I'm coming as fast as I can."

"What are you up to Sam?" asked his grandfather.

"I'm looking for my notes about the War of American Independence," said Sam, "they're here somewhere... found them!" he soon called out.

"O.K. let's begin with you Sam; I think you were going to find out the dates of the war for me... what were those?"

Sam looked at his notes. "1775 to 1783. Actually our government decided to end the war in 1782, but it took almost a year to sign the peace documents."

"Very good; now how about you Nikki, can you tell me the answer to the second question?"

"Yes, Grandpa, it was General George Washington."

"Excellent. Of course, not all the English settlers in the colonies approved of the war against their home country and so almost one hundred thousand of them decided to leave and start their lives again in Canada and a new colony was created for them in 1784 called New Brunswick."

"It seems that the war in America went on for quite a long time, Grandpa; did the colonists have any help from any other country?" asked Sam.

"Yes they did, the French were quick to take advantage of the situation to assist them against England, and without the help of the French forces it is possible the colonists would have lost," replied his grandfather.

"... but you said that George III had a new peace treaty with France," said Nikki.

"Yes there was a treaty, but the French King Louis XVI and his ministers, could not resist the chance of helping anyone who was willing to attack England, even though the cost to their country was enormous. The French involvement in the American War of Independence led directly to the beginnings of a revolution in France against Louis; he and his queen were eventually executed by the French people in 1793."

"Wow! That didn't do him much good then," said Sam.

"No, it certainly did not. However, in spite of the various conflicts, the last years of the 18th Century were times of great change and exploration for the English nation. Back in 1771 Captain Cook had discovered Australia, and in India, the East India Company had acquired almost by mistake, vast new territories. In England itself a very different sort of revolution was starting... the Industrial

St Cuthbert's, Marston near Middlesborough. The place of baptism of Captain James Cook.

Revolution. Water power and steam power were beginning to transform the making of almost everything that had previously been made by hand. For example, the making of cast iron was made much more efficient and so men began to visualise making huge structures with it. The first iron bridge in

The iron bridge at Ironbridge

the world was built in Shropshire over the River Severn gorge in 1779 and it is still in position today... would you believe the place is called Ironbridge!"

"It seems as if 'England's Story' is becoming much more complicated," said Nikki.

"Of course you are quite right, but I'll try and make it as simple as I can," replied her grandfather. "To remind you, we are still in the reign of George III and I've got another two names for you to remember... one was William Pitt, the son of the first William Pitt. He was the new Prime Minister in 1783 — he was the youngest Prime Minister we have ever had; he was just twenty-four — and the other was John Wesley the founder of a new way of religious expression called Methodism. Both of these men had a strong effect on the life of our nation."

"How, Grandpa?" asked Sam.

"William Pitt managed to restore the financial strength of the country after the war against the American colonists, and John Wesley, whom I've mentioned before, managed to introduce a form of religious observance, to which the great mass of the new industrial workers could respond and understand. Both of them in different ways aimed to create a sense of peace and stability in a turbulent world, for in Europe the scale and hideousness of the French Revolution was a worry to all countries. After Louis XVI and his queen had been executed, the revolutionaries in France declared war on England and just about everyone else, and that was how it was for the next twenty years or so."

"Do you mean that England and France were at war for the whole of that time?" asked Nikki.

"For most of the time, and partly because a new leader called Napoleon Bonaparte came to power in France. Have you heard of Napoleon?"

"Yes, " said Sam, "he was a famous general I think."

" ... and very successful too. He eventually made himself Emperor of France and most of Europe as well; the only country that defied his forces was England."

"Did he try to invade England?" asked Nikki.

"He certainly planned to do so, but after Admiral Lord Nelson and the Royal Navy defeated the combined fleets of France and Spain at the Battle of Trafalgar in 1805, he had no means of bringing his vast armies across the English Channel."

"I remember that Lord Nelson died during the battle," said Sam

Nelson's Column, Trafalgar Square, London

quietly."Isn't there a Nelson's Column in London?"

"There is, and as I'm sure you know it stands in Trafalgar Square."

" I remember that the name of Nelson's ship was 'H.M.S. Victory'," said Nikki, "and you can still see it today in a dry-dock at Portsmouth."

"Absolutely correct... that's another place we must take you," said her grandfather.

"We've actually been there with our school," said Sam, "but I would love to go again, there is so much to see there."

"Can you take us on the boat trip around the harbour again, please, Grandpa?" asked Nikki, "I did enjoy that!"

"I'm sure we can," replied her grandfather, "but now we must return to the reign of George III. Do you remember we spoke about the Prime Minister William Pitt?"

"Yes, Grandpa... the youngest one there has ever been."

"Well, I have to tell you that he died very young too, at the age of forty-seven, in 1806."

"What did King George do?"

"Luckily, he was able to find different politicians to carry on the government and fight the war, but in 1810 the King became very ill and so his son George became Regent."

"Excuse me, but what does 'regent' mean?" asked Sam.

"I will explain that next time Sam, because our story now moves into the nineteenth century and this is a good place to pause for a while."

"When can we come again?" asked Nikki,

"How about next Wednesday?"

"I think that will be fine," said Sam.

CHAPTER 16

THE 19th CENTURY

George IV 1820–1830
William IV 1830–1837
Queen Victoria 1837–1901
England becomes a world power

BJB

Next Wednesday soon came.

Sam had remembered his question from last time...

"Please could you start by explaining what a 'regent ' was?" he asked.

"Of course, a Regent is a person who is permitted by parliament to carry out the duties of the monarch. George III's son became known as 'The Prince Regent'. At about this time, the British government realised that if Napoleon was to be defeated, a war would have to be fought in Europe once again, and they appointed a very brilliant general, the Duke of Wellington, to command the forces against Napoleon. In 1815 at the famous Battle of Waterloo, the Duke of Wellington and the British army, helped by the armies of the Dutch and the Prussians, was finally victorious. Peace came to Europe at last. "

A Waterloo Medal

"What happened to Napoleon Grandpa?" asked Nikki.

"He escaped from the battlefield and later surrendered to the captain of a Royal Navy ship, who brought him to England. The government sent him to be imprisoned as far away from Europe as possible, on the British island of St. Helena in the southern Atlantic Ocean. He died there in 1821."

"Did George III ever get better, Grandpa?" asked Sam.

"No, I'm afraid he did not, he died in 1820 and the Prince Regent then became king in his own right as King George IV. It was during his reign in 1825 that the first passenger railway was built from Stockton to Darlington in northern England."

"I think the engine was called the Rocket, wasn't it?" said Sam.

"No I'm afraid you're wrong this time, it was called 'Locomotion No. 1' but it was built by the same father and son who did build the 'Rocket', they were George and Robert Stephenson."

"Do you mean it was the first passenger railway in the whole world?" asked Nikki.

Locomotion No. 1

"Yes it was, and for the next thirty years all the railways built anywhere in the world were built by British engineers. This was the time of other "firsts" also... Sir Robert Peel, who later became a Prime Minister, created the first proper police force in London at Scotland Yard in 1829; their headquarters is still in the same place today [some people still call policemen 'bobbies" after the shortened version of his Christian name]. The first horse bus service began in London in the same year, but of course most people still travelled around England by stagecoach."

"What sort of roads did they have in those days, Grandpa?" asked Sam.

"Not very good ones by the standards of today. There had been a fairly good network of turnpikes since about 1770, and bit by bit there were other improvements like private canals to transport coal for the new iron works etc."

" Excuse me, Grandpa, but what was a turnpike?" asked Nikki.

"It was a privately made road, which was allowed to charge travellers who used it; the turnpike itself was the name of the spiked barrier which was opened once people had paid their money. A famous engineer of this

The Menai Bridge of Thomas Telford

time, whom you may have heard about and who built roads, bridges and canals was Thomas Telford. There is now a town named after him in Shropshire. The bridge he built to join Wales to the Island of Anglesey was opened in 1826, it was the first suspension bridge in the world."

"What is a suspension bridge?" asked Sam.

"What does the word sound like to you? You should be able to work it out."

"Hanging?"

"Yes, the deck of the bridge is hung or suspended rather than being built on stone arches. These days it is usually supported on ropes of steel between two supports on either side of the valley or river which is to be crossed, but I think Mr.Telford used chains on his bridge. However, in 1824 a new London Bridge was started, which crossed the River Thames on arches in the usual way."

"Was this to replace the old one which had houses on it?" asked Nikki.

"Yes it was; the old one had shops and a chapel as well as houses and also a place where the heads of traitors were displayed after their execution."

"How horrid!" exclaimed Nikki, "I don't think I should have liked walking there."

"How old was the old bridge?" asked Sam.

"It was built in 1209, but there were earlier bridges... remember we said that the Romans probably built the first one."

"Did George IV open the new London Bridge?" asked Nikki.

"No, I'm afraid not, he died in 1830, and the new bridge was opened in 1831 by his successor, William IV, who was his brother."

"That must mean that George IV had no children," said Sam.

"Actually, he did once have a daughter, Princess Charlotte, but she had died in 1817, and it was the daughter of another of his brothers that eventually became Queen Victoria after William IV died."

"Do you know what happened to the Duke of Wellington?" asked Sam.

"Yes I do, he actually became Prime Minister for George IV in 1828, but when William IV succeeded to the throne, there was an election and a new governing party took control of Parliament. He stayed on as Commander-in-Chief of the army and died in 1852."

"Were the political parties the same as today?" asked Nikki, "always arguing and changing things."

"Yes, more or less... and of course things do need changing from time to time. In those days not many people were allowed to vote, but more and more people wanted to have a chance to choose their M.P.s. It was a scandal that often the new industrial towns like Manchester had no M.P.s, whilst some places with no people had two!"

"Gosh that sounds very unfair," said Nikki.

"It was, so the new government of William IV passed a Reform Act in 1832, which made everything much fairer and allowed more people to vote. During the rest of the century this process continued and England began to become a democracy, leading the world in this sort of government."

"I'm sorry to ask another question," said Nikki, "but what exactly is democracy?"

"It is a form of government that allows all the adult people of a country to have an equal say in electing their representatives to a parliament where the laws are made."

"Thank you, Grandpa."

"Did King William reign for very long?" asked Sam.

"No, just seven years."

"So that means Princess Victoria became Queen in 1837," said Nikki.

"Yes that's right, and she was just eighteen years old."

"Did she have any problems with her uncles," said Sam with a little smile.

"No, I don't think so, although there were three of them still alive. However, one thing she was determined to do, was to set high standards of royal behaviour and make a complete change from the poor example of her uncles... particularly George IV."

"Who did she marry, Grandpa?" asked Nikki.

"She married a German prince, called Albert, in February 1840; they had nine children and were very happy together until Prince Albert died suddenly in 1861. Eventually all her children married into other European royal families and she became known as the 'grandmother of Europe'."

"Did she always live in Buckingham Palace or Windsor Castle?" asked Sam.

"No, she had other homes that I think she preferred, one in Scotland called 'Balmoral Castle' and another in the Isle of Wight called 'Osborne House'."

Osborne House, Isle of Wight

"Were there any wars during her reign?" asked Nikki.

"There were some of course, but the Prime Ministers who controlled things tried to avoid them as far as possible. Other European nations spent quite a bit of the century fighting each other, or struggling with revolutions, even the U.S.A. had a civil war from 1861–1865. Whilst these sorts of conflicts were going on, Britain gradually acquired an enormous empire of territories all around the world, and there were few places where the British did not exercise control or great influence. Today's modern world began in Queen Victoria's reign and resulted in English becoming the most important language to know, in most parts of the world."

"What modern things do you mean, Grandpa?" asked Sam.

"Well for example, in 1840, the world's first photograph was taken in England; the world's first postal service was organised here in the same year, with the world's first postage stamps. The world's first trade exhibition, sponsored by Prince Albert was held in London in 1851, in what was known as the Crystal Palace, an amazing building made almost entirely of glass. The world's first underground railway opened in London in 1863. In science, art, architecture, literature and education Britain led the world during the 19th century, and I expect if I mention some of the famous names of that time, you can tell me what they were famous for... shall we try?"

The world's first photograph was made here at Lacock Abbey

The world's first stamps 'Penny Blacks'

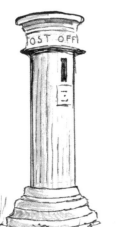

Victorian pillarbox at Mudeford, Hampshire

"Oh yes, Grandpa, that **will** be fun."

"First one then... Charles Darwin."

"Umm...Science?"

"Good. Next one...John Constable."

"Painting pictures."

"Very good... let me see... how about Charles Dickens?"

"I think it was stories," said Nikki.

"Yes it was, he wrote many stories, mostly so that his readers would become aware of the lives of poor people at that time; I think he hoped that by doing so, Parliament would make laws to improve the conditions in which the poor people lived. Now for another one... Florence Nightingale."

"That's easy, ... Nursing"

"Yes of course . Here's one perhaps a bit more difficult...Isambard Brunel."

The children looked at each other glumly and replied, "We don't know him."

"Let me tell you then, that he was a great engineer, who is famous for building the Great Western Railway from London to Bristol, as well as the world's first iron-hulled, steam-powered ship called the S.S. Great Britain, which was launched in 1843."

"A friend of mine has been to see it I think," said Sam.

"Quite possibly, because it is on display in Bristol," replied his grandfather.

The world's first tunnel under a river by Brunel

"Isambard doesn't sound like an English name," said Nikki,

"No, it wasn't; his father was a Frenchman, who went to America to escape the horrors of the French Revolution and then later he came to London. It was Mr. Brunel, who, helped by his son, built the first tunnel under the River Thames in London during the years 1825 until 1843."

"There seems to have been an awful lot happening in England during Queen Victoria's reign, said Sam, "and you did say there were some wars... when did they happen?"

"The Crimean War began in 1853 against Russia, and the war against the Boers in South Africa in 1899; my grandfather was a soldier in the Royal Berkshire Regiment, and he fought in the Boer War."

"Wow!"

" The most beneficial thing that came from the experiences of the Crimean War, was the development of nursing services. To start with it was mainly for sick and wounded soldiers but the new practices gradually spread to benefit all the people."

"How long did the Crimean War last?" asked Nikki.

"Only about two years."

"Where is Crimea?"

1.ENGLAND
2.FRANCE
3.SPAIN
4.ITALY
5.GREECE
6.RUSSIA
7.The CRIMEA

BLACK SEA

The Crimean War Map... the European countries

"It's that part of Russia that sticks out into the Black Sea... bring me the atlas and I'll show you where it is."

"Why did we fight a war there?" asked Sam as he looked at the map.

"It is very complicated, but it had its origins in a dispute between Napoleon III, the Emperor of France, who was the nephew of the first Napoleon we mentioned, and the Czar of Russia about the protection of Christians in the Holy Land, which then was controlled by the Muslim Turkish Empire... we were on the side of France. Our government was worried also about the Russians trying to upset our control of India."

"Was India still under the control of the East India Company," asked Nikki.

"It was, until there was a mutiny by some of the company's Indian soldiers in 1857, whereupon our government took full control of the country by an act of Parliament in 1858. The Act became a sort of Magna Carta for India, and some years later Queen Victoria was given the title of Empress of India. Perhaps the most important thing was that the Act recognised that someday India would rule itself, as it now does."

"What was the other war you mentioned Grandpa," asked Sam.

"The Boer War, or perhaps I should say 'the war against the Boers'."

"Who were they?"

"They were the descendants of the original Dutch settlers in South Africa and they resented the British authority over them, which had started after the war against Napoleon Bonaparte one hundred years earlier. There was also the fact that the British probably wanted control over the large deposits of gold and diamonds which had recently been found in South Africa."

"What did your grandfather do in the Boer War, Grandpa?" asked Nikki.

"It would be easy to say 'his duty, for he was only a soldier of low rank. After two years in South Africa he became very sick and was sent home to England. He arrived home just before Queen Victoria died in 1901."

English soldiers in the Boer War

"It was whilst he was recovering in hospital at Reading that he met my grandmother, your great-great grandmother, and they were married in 1905."

"I'm glad about that," said Nikki, "but where did Queen Victoria die Grandpa?"

"In Osborne House, which, of course, was her home on the Isle of Wight. Her coffin lay in state in the dining room at Osborne, until her body was taken to Windsor via London for her state funeral. However, it was in the 'royal' church in the village of Whippingham that the royal family always attended church services when in residence at Osborne ."

St Mildred's Whippingham, Isle of Wight

Prince Albert, the Queen's husband, helped with the redesign of the church to make it more suitable for royal use, and because they always spent Christmas at Osborne I think it was his idea that it became the first church in England to have central heating."

"That was nice for everyone," said Sam. "I suppose the Queen must have been quite old when she died."

" She was eighty-one and had reigned for sixty-four years; the longest time of any monarch up to now."

"Who came after her?" asked Sam.

"Her eldest son, Albert, the Prince of Wales, chose to be called by his

125

second name as Edward VII, and very quickly after his accession the war in South Africa ended."

"Weren't there really any other wars except the Boer War and the Crimean War?" asked Sam.

"Well, there were one or two minor ones, for example, on the north-west frontier of India and in Africa. A young officer named Winston Churchill whose name I'm sure you remember..."

..."Born in Blenheim Palace," said Sam.

"Yes, that's right. Well, he managed to use his family connections to take part in both the campaigns and made a name for himself by writing books about the wars, as well as articles for newspapers to tell the people at home in England what it was like. After leaving the army he became a member of parliament and eventually he was our Prime Minister during the second World War... he was also quite an accomplished artist."

"Gosh, he did a lot in his life didn't he?"said Nikki.

"He certainly did!"

"Was Edward VII a good king?" she asked.

"I think I must ask you to pose that question again when we next meet, because..."

... "Oh, all right Grandpa, but can I just ask if it's true that England's Story is now going to be more about ordinary people than about kings and queens, and even parliaments?"

"I suppose it is, but you must try to be patient and I will definitely answer both your questions when next time we meet, because we have now reached the twentieth century and this is a good place for us to pause."

"Of course I do understand Grandpa, thank you... it is all very interesting," she added.

Queen Victoria's favourite silver crown.
It was just 10cms in diameter and contained 1187 separate diamonds.
It was placed upon her coffin after her death in Osborne House.

CHAPTER 17

THE 20th CENTURY

The World Wars
Edward VII 1901–1910
George V 1910–1936
Edward VIII 1936
George VI 1936–1952

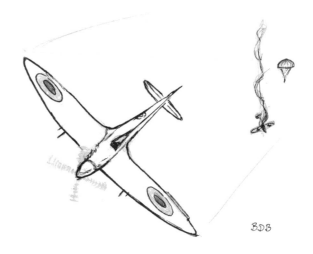

BDB

"Well here we are again," said the twins grandfather, "If I remember correctly Nikki, last time you were asking if England's Story is more about ordinary people than kings and parliaments and if Edward VII was a good king?"

"Yes, Grandpa."

"I will answer the second question first, for it rather depends on what we mean by 'good'; I think Edward VII was a friendly and mostly kind man who indulged himself in what we might call 'the pleasures of life'. He was happy to allow his ministers to deal with all the difficult problems of running the country, and we could say that the world changed around him, without him really bothering. As to your second question, I would say you are probably right. It was the spread of the English language and the British way of life to so many countries of the world by ordinary people, that now takes over as an important part of our story as a nation. During this story I've mentioned how certain freedoms were won by Englishmen from their rulers; it was these sorts of freedoms we encouraged other people to want for themselves... for example, the freedom to say what we think and believe, and to argue our differences in democratic councils and parliaments. The British fought two world wars in the 20th century to maintain such beliefs, the first of which happened very soon after Edward VII died."

"Grandpa, you mentioned lots of changes happened during Edward VII's reign," said Sam, "What kind of changes were they, Grandpa?"

"Well, the year of his accession to the throne [1901] was the year that

Mr. Marconi sent the first radio Morse code signals from Cornwall across the Atlantic Ocean to Newfoundland. The next year Mrs. Pankhurst began an organisation to seek votes for women. In 1903 came the first flight of a powered aircraft by the Wright brothers in America and then those flying experiments were copied in other countries as well. The first flight in England was at

M. Bleriot is first to fly across the English Channel 1909

Farnborough on 16th October 1908. Amazingly, just one year later a Frenchman, Monsieur Bleriot, became the first man to fly his tiny aircraft across the English Channel. These were also the years when motor cars began to replace horses in all the industrialised countries, and in 1904 the first Rolls Royce car was built."

"They are the most expensive cars in the world, aren't they Grandpa?" said Sam.

"I think that today there may be one or two that are a bit more expensive, but certainly no name has a greater prestige."

"What is prestige?"

A Rolls Royce car of 1904

"When talking about cars, I would say it means having a reputation for reliability and the very highest quality."

"Did Mrs Pankhurst manage to get votes for women?" asked Nikki.

"No, I'm afraid that did not happen until after the end of the first World War."

"When was that war Grandpa, and when did the king die?"

"The First World War, sometimes called The Great War, began in 1914. King Edward VII died in 1910 and Florence Nightingale died the same year."

"Is she buried with all the other famous people in Westminster Abbey?" asked Nikki.

"No, she requested that her burial place should be near her home in East Wellow in Hampshire, which is not far from Southampton and the New Forest."

"Who became the next king? " asked Nikki.

"As you might expect, it was Edward's eldest son; he chose to be called George V. Unfortunately, at the time he succeeded to the throne, there was a dispute in Parliament between the House of Commons and the House of Lords as to which should have the final say about new laws. The Prime Minister, Mr. Asquith, felt that he had the support of the new king and so the House of Commons won the argument. As I have already said, George V became king at a time when many people realised there could be a war with Germany."

"Why did they think that?"

"Well, the German king or 'Kaiser' as he was called, wanted Germany to have a strong army, and also a navy as powerful as the Royal Navy of Britain. Our government felt equally strongly that we should always have more ships than the Germans because of our links across the seas with the countries of our empire, so there was an 'arms race' to see who could build the most battleships."

"Who won?"

"Neither country, because the war broke out in 1914 anyway, for a different reason entirely."

"I've heard about 'The Great War'," said Sam, "and how awful it was, and I know it lasted four years because I've seen the dates on our war memorial; but we did win in the end didn't we?"

Some British Dreadnought battleships of 1910

"Yes, we did, but remember we were one of seven countries fighting as allies together and from April 1917 the Americans sent soldiers to help us too."

"How did it end, Grandpa?"

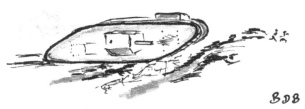

A British Army tank of 1917

"The allied soldiers fighting in Belgium and France used their secret weapons, the tanks, and with them at last they could drive over all the barbed-wire and the thousands of trenches that the soldiers on both sides had dug to protect themselves from shell fire. In this way they finally overcame the German armies and the Germans asked for a stop to the war. It was agreed that all fighting should stop at 11 o'clock on the morning of the 11th November, which as you know is the eleventh month, in the year 1918. Ever since then 11th November has been called Remembrance Day and as you know, we remember all who died fighting for our country in the Great War and all wars since, with parades and church services at the war memorials."

"Was your grandfather in the Great War as well as in the Boer War?" asked Nikki.

Keston, Kent. The village war memorial

130

"Yes he was. He suffered greatly from his experiences in the trenches, and in 1916 he was discharged from the army for medical reasons. His name appears on the war memorial of the village of Keston in Kent where he lived with his family after his time in the army. He died a fortnight after the war ended."

"So he <u>did</u> know that the war was over?"

"Yes."

"I'm glad. Then what happened?"

"In England, do you mean?"

"Yes."

"Well, the war had cost a lot of money and a lot of lives. The forces of the British Empire were about 10 million men, of whom about 1 million died and another 2 million were wounded. One of the biggest problems with which all the allied governments had to deal, was the troops all wanted to be discharged from their service as quickly as possible and go to their homes."

"Was there any work for them to do?"

"Not enough."

"Did the Germans have to pay for the damage the war had caused?"

World War I cemetery in France

"Yes, the Peace Treaty demanded that they must make payments in lands and money, and never again be allowed to have sufficient forces to start another war, but as the years went by the Germans ignored the treaty. In the mean time, in 1920, most of the countries of the world agreed to set up an organisation called the League of Nations, where it was hoped that disputes between countries could be resolved without starting wars. Unfortunately, the nation that was becoming the most important nation in the world at that time, the USA, did not join, and Germany and Russia were not allowed to join."

"Why was that, Grandpa?"

"Germany as a punishment for starting the war, and Russia because in 1917 there had been a revolution, won by the communists, who had murdered all of the former Russian royal family."

"Was our country a member of the League of Nations?"

"Yes it was, but our government had many other things to attend to, particularly the problems between the inhabitants of Ireland, which had been getting worse for years. Eventually in 1922, Ireland was divided up into Northern Ireland and the larger southern part, became the Irish Free State."

"Was it because they wanted to be independent of England?" asked Sam.

"Yes, for those in southern Ireland it was, and other countries of the British Empire wanted the same, particularly India. In 1930 a man named Gandhi organised protest marches against the British."

Gandhi leads a protest in India

"Did the Indians get their wish?"

"No, not until 1948, after the next World War."

"What about all the other countries in the Empire?"

"In 1931, all the largest and oldest countries, like Canada and Australia etc., became what were called Independent Dominions."

"Was there much empire left after that?" asked Nikki.

"Oh, yes, there was still quite a bit, I can assure you," replied her grandfather, "and at this same time an association of the newly independent states was formed called 'The Commonwealth of Nations' or 'The British Commonwealth'; now today there are 53 members including most of the former colonies of the Empire."

"What does 'commonwealth' mean?"

"I think it is quite a good word, because it means believing in certain common standards of law and justice and having a care for each other's wellbeing. It turned out to be very necessary, because in Germany a new leader called Adolf Hitler came to power in 1933, and he began to create a new army, navy and air force, and took no notice of the old peace treaty. He tried to blame all Germany's troubles on people of the Jewish faith living in Germany. He soon became a very dangerous leader indeed and it was he and his Nazi Party, who caused the Second World War."

"Was George V still alive at this time, Grandpa?"

"Yes he was, but he actually died on my birthday, 20th January 1936."

"Wow, that's interesting! Who came next?" asked Nikki.

"George V's eldest son, The Prince of Wales, became Edward VIII, but his was one of the shortest reigns in our history. It was less than a year."

"Why was that?"

"He had fallen in love with a twice-divorced American lady; the government and many ordinary people felt she was unsuitable to be Queen. When this was explained to King Edward by the Prime Minister, he decided to abdicate, which means 'give up the throne', in order to marry her. The next person in line to the throne was his brother, the Duke of York. He chose the title of George VI; fortunately he was already married and had two daughters. His reign started in a time of peace, but like his father George V, only a few years went by before Britain was once again involved fighting a war against Germany, this time the Germans were soon joined by Italy and Japan."

"Why did the war begin Grandpa?" asked Sam.

"Because the German government, under the leadership of Adolf Hitler, invaded Poland trying to get more land. Britain and France had promised to protect Poland from any German invasion... so in September 1939 we went to war against Germany on behalf of the Polish people."

"How long did that war last?"

"Six years. After capturing Poland, Hitler sent the German armies into Belgium and France and soon both countries surrendered and although we eventually won with support from the countries of the Commonwealth and Russia, it would have lasted much longer if we had not had the help once again of the USA from 1942. It was truly a World War for we had to try to protect not only our own country by waging war in Europe , but also to fight the Japanese and Italians to preserve our influence in India, Burma, and in North Africa."

"How did it end?"

"First of all Italy was defeated in 1943 and then Germany in 1945;[Adolf Hitler committed suicide in his headquarters in Berlin] a short while later, after the dropping of the new secret 'atom bomb' on Japan, the Emperor of Japan also surrendered all his forces, and the war was over."

The first atomic bomb is dropped on Hiroshima

"What happened to you during the war, Grandpa?" asked Nikki.

"Lots of things, most of which I will tell you about another day, but you might like to know that when I was five I remember the night a bomb dropped on a house across the road from ours, and our house was so badly damaged that we could no longer live there." "What did you do?"

"My Granny took me to live with friends on a farm in Somerset."

"Was that what they call evac..u..ation?" asked Nikki, as she tried to remember the right word.

"Yes it was, but my father and mother arranged everything, and soon we all lived together again in Oxted in Surrey. The RAF patched up our house and used it for people from Biggin Hill airfield for the rest of the war. Biggin hill was very famous for its role during the Battle of Britain in 1940, when all that stopped the Germans invading our country were the fighter pilots ofthe RAF."

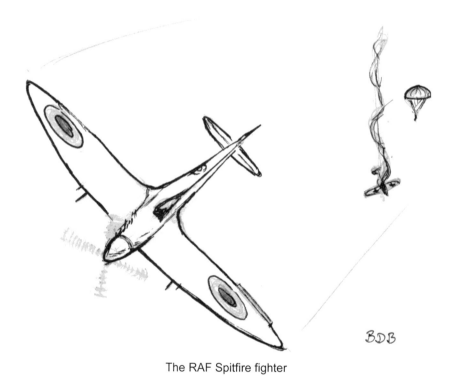

BDB

The RAF Spitfire fighter

"Did you see Spitfires and tanks and things?" asked Sam.

"Oh, yes... and prisoners of war working in the fields, and the German V1 rocket bombs, which we called 'doddlebugs'."

"Did you see Winston Churchill too?" asked Nikki.

"No, not then, but after the war when I went to school in London, I did see him once in a car. He was a very great war leader, as well as an author and artist."

"What was it like then after the war was over?" asked Sam.

"Things got better very slowly; to start with, food was still in short supply and millions of people all over the world were homeless, nearly every European city was damaged in some serious way.

The victorious nations set up new friendly governments in all the old enemy countries and created a new organisation called the United Nations to deal with any future disputes. In our own country laws were made giving independence to India and many other former parts of the British Empire. Sadly, immediately after the war was over, a new threat to world peace came from our former ally Russia, which had a communist dictatorship. The threat of Russian military action affected the entire world until the end of the 20th century. The democratic nations felt that to protect and keep their freedom, they had to fight wars or prepare to fight wars against communism."

St Paul's Cathedral during the 'blitz' on London, 1941

"How did they do that, Grandpa?" asked Nikki.

"An important alliance was made called N.A.T.O. [the North Atlantic Treaty Organisation]. This included our country, the U.S.A., Canada and most other European countries, who said that if Russia (U.S.S.R.) attacked any of them, it would be considered to be an attack on all of them; in other words they would all help each other."

"Was it successful?" asked Sam.

"Yes it was, there was no actual fighting between N.A.T.O. and U.S.S.R.... the Cold War, as it was known, lasted for about forty years until the U.S.S.R. broke apart into separate countries in December 1991."

"Gosh that was a long time," said Nikki, then she added, "Did we mind not having an empire after the war, Grandpa?"

"No not really, we were no longer a rich nation and we soon realised that giving independence to our old colonies was best for them and good for us too."

"What about King George VI," asked Nikki, "we seem to have forgotten about him."

"He did very well, in spite of being a very shy man, he and his queen did not hesitate to do all they could to help in the war effort, and to support our famous Prime Minister, Winston Churchill, in his task of leading the nation throughout the war. Sadly the strain of the king's responsibilities brought about his early death in 1952 and then his eldest daughter Elizabeth became our Queen Elizabeth II. On the day of her coronation in 1953, it was announced that two members of a British expedition had at last climbed the highest mountain in the world, Mount Everest. One was Edmund Hillary a New Zealander, and the other was his climbing companion, a man from Nepal called Tenzing Norgay."

"Gosh that was quite exciting wasn't it?" said Nikki.

"Indeed it was. In England people talked about a new 'Elizabethan Age' beginning."

Mount Everest first climbed by Hilary and Tenzing, 1953

CHAPTER 18

THE 20th & 21st CENTURIES

Towards the future
Queen Elizabeth II
1952–Present day

"What was the biggest change from before the war to after the war, Grandpa?" asked Sam.

"I expect different people would say different things, but I believe it was the changes in the realms of air warfare and air transport. Just about the time the war was beginning, a Royal Air Force officer called Frank Whittle invented the jet engine, and although it took almost to the end of the war before these engines were actually used in aircraft, as soon as the war ended the new engines were gradually put into civilian transport planes, the first of which was the British De Havilland 'Comet'.

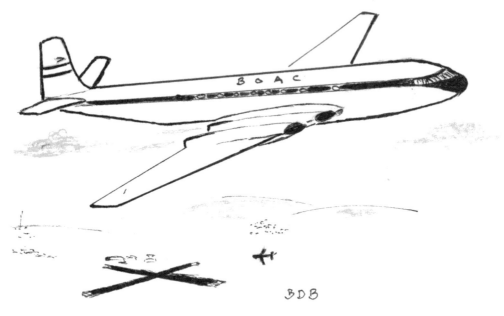

The Comet. The world's first jet airliner

3D8

The Concorde. The world's first supersonic airliner

Within twenty years almost every aircraft was powered by jet engines and as the speed of travel increased and the cost of flying reduced, everyone who wanted to do so, was able to travel abroad for their holidays. By 1969 the British and French governments had managed to finance the building of the Concorde supersonic airliner, which was able to fly faster than a rifle bullet."

"Wow!"

"As well as developments in the air there was also the exploration of space going on at the same time. In the same year, the amazing feat of sending men to land on the moon was finally accomplished by the United States government. Two astronauts, of which Neil Armstrong was the first, stepped on to the moon's surface and just as remarkably, successfully returned to Earth. The enormous rockets that the Americans used to put 'man' into space, were developed from the rockets that the Germans used to bomb England during the war."

"What did they find on the moon, Grandpa?" asked Sam.

"Not a lot... some samples of moon rocks were brought back to Earth but, so far, they have proved to have little value."

"Did we make rockets too?"

"Yes, a few, but it was too expensive for our country to try to copy America and Russia, who had become the most powerful nations."

"Were there still wars in other places?"

"Yes, I'm afraid there were; usually our soldiers were part of the United Nations forces but there were terrorist actions in Northern Ireland that began in 1969 and lasted for about thirty years. Sadly, there are always some people who think they can solve problems and make the world a better place by killing other people, which is of course, rubbish! Three years after Britain had elected our country's first woman Prime Minister Mrs. Thatcher in 1979, the Argentine forces invaded the British territory of the Falkland Islands, and we had to send soldiers, sailors and airmen to win them back."

138

"How long did that war last?"

"Not very long, only about three months. In spite of all these things happening Britain gradually became a more prosperous country. It was not long after the Second World War finished that television sets began to appear in most homes, and ordinary people could afford cars. The first motorways were built and lots of less important railway lines were closed because nobody used them anymore."

British troops in the Falkland Island war 1982

"I know an old railway track that is now a footpath," said Nikki.

"I think I know the one you mean, you can still see some of the old bridges," replied her grandfather.

"Did people still build new bridges in the 20th century?"

"Oh yes! Bridges had to be built to carry the new motorways over the same estuaries that the older railway bridges had crossed a hundred years before, I remember flying my helicopter

'I know an old railway track that is now a footpath'

and taking part in a 'flypast' to mark the opening of the new Forth Road Bridge in September 1964. Over the River Severn eventually two new separate bridges had to be built to carry the volume of traffic across that estuary between England and Wales."

RAF helicopter over the Forth road bridge

"An estuary is where a river meets the sea, isn't it Grandpa?" said Sam.

"Yes it is; and we must not forget tunnels too! The most famous of course is the Channel Tunnel linking England to France.

139

Euro Tunnel entrance at Folkestone, Kent

This was begun in 1988 and finished in 1994; new underground railway tunnels were also built under London in 1970 and 1977."

"What other new things were there at that time?"

"Well, people of my generation would probably call the second half of the 20th century the beginning of the Information and Communications Revolution, because mobile phones and personal computers became more and more the normal things for people to use. At the same time scientists became concerned about 'climate change' due, it was thought, to pollution from industrial processes and car exhausts. Of course the world's climate is always changing — it's not a new thing — and there were no cars or industries during the last 'warm period' 20,000 years ago, but it is good that we are all learning to be more careful with the precious resources of our planet. The biggest problem for future generations to think about, will be the actual numbers of people in the world, and how to control them."

"It sounds as if our story has changed from being 'England's Story' to being 'Britain's Story', and now it is becoming 'The World's Story'!" said Sam.

"In a way you are correct, now that our small country is part of the European Union, but at the same time people do like to be part of smaller groups too. For example, as the century came to its end in 1999, the Welsh and Scottish people of Britain took the first steps to taking some decisions for themselves when the Welsh Assembly and the Scottish Parliament were created, so perhaps England will one day again be back to being a country on its own... I must say I hope not. Of course each of the nations of Great Britain has always had its own sports teams and England is especially famous for giving the game of cricket to the world and of course England won the football World Cup in 1966."

"But not when it comes to the Olympics... remember 2012 and 'TEAM GB', and how well all the people did to win their medals," said Sam. "It would be a pity if that all changed."

"But what makes England on its own important today?" asked Nikki.

"For a start, many people would say that London is the financial capital of the world with all its banks and insurance companies, and we are rightly proud of our democratic form of government with The Queen as Head of State. We can be equally proud of our artists, musicians, our medical scientists and our steadily evolving educational system. We remain as one of the five permanent members of the United Nations Security Council, so our opinions matter around the world, and British people are still great inventors... don't forget that Sir Tim Berners-Lee was the inventor of the World Wide Web, and we have our own satellite companies too you know.

Hylas 2 satellite of Avanti Communications

Our engineers and other scientists continue to build amazing buildings and make wonderful discoveries and our people in general are among the most generous in the world in giving to charities... I could go on, but I think that's enough. We are coming to the end of my story, but England's Story will not stop. It will be your generation that will write the next page of our history, and if you build on our rich heritage by learning lessons from the past that we have tried to understand together, then, I'm sure in the words of a song 'There'll always be an England...' and we can all face the future with great confidence."

"Thank you, Grandpa... we did enjoy the story."

"Before we finish, I would just like you both to read something for me... it's from Shakespeare's play Richard II, and spoken by John of Gaunt the Duke of Lancaster... let me find the place. Would you like to start Nikki?"

"Yes, I don't mind but I'm not very good."

"Just read it quite slowly... I think you will enjoy the words; it's all about England."

> NIKKI... "*This royal throne of kings, this scepter'd isle,*
> *This earth of majesty, this seat of Mars,*
> *This other Eden, demi-paradise*
> *This fortress built by nature for herself*
> *Against infection and the hand of war...*"

"Now you please carry on Sam."

> SAM... "*This happy breed of men, this little world,*
> *This precious stone set in the silver sea,*
> *Which serves it in the office of a wall,*
> *Or as a moat defensive to a house,*
> *Against the envy of less happier lands,*
> *This blessed plot, this earth, this realm, this England...*"

"There is more as you can see, but we'll stop there... well done both of you."

"That was fun, Grandpa. Can we read some more Shakespeare another day?" asked Nikki, "is that really the end of England's Story?"

"I'm afraid so. I hope you will be able to remember it... or some of it!"

"Can you write it all down for us...the whole story I mean... perhaps one day quite soon?"

"Well, there's a thought. Perhaps I <u>will</u> try to do that... now off you go."

THE END

Portsmouth Harbour
Hampshire
Once the home of the Roman fleet at Portchester Castle,
Portsmouth has been the home of the British fleet since the middle ages.
In this photograph can be seen HMS Warrior launched in 1860, now a museum,
and two modern Royal Naval ships, HMS Defender and HMS Iron Duke.

HMS Iron Duke | HMS Defender